Pop/Rock Piano Hits FOR DUMMIES®

Performance Notes by Robbie Gennet

ISBN 1-4234-0775-X

HAL•LEONARD®
CORPORATION
7777 W. BLUEMOUND RD. P.O. BOX 13819 MILWAUKEE, WI 53213

Visit Hal Leonard Online at
www.halleonard.com

Table of Contents

Introduction

Welcome to *Pop/Rock Piano Hits for Dummies!* You'll find everything you need to play some of the greatest and most popular rock songs, including piano/vocal arrangements of the songs and performance notes that will help you through them. And you don't need a music degree to understand the terms.

About This Book

The music in this book is in standard piano notation — a staff for the melody and lyrics above the traditional piano grand staff. Above everything you will find the basic chords and their matching guitar frames. The frames are diagrams of the guitar strings that show you what frets to play. Even though this book features songs that sound great on piano, I assume you or a friend may also want to learn the accompanying guitar part. I also assume you know a little something about reading music, and that you know a little bit about playing piano (and possibly guitar) — like how to hold your fingers, basic chords, and how to look cool while doing it. If you need a refresher course on piano basics, please check out *Piano For Dummies*, by Blake Neely (Wiley).

How to Use This Book

For every song, I give you a brief intro with a little background on the artist (in case you're not already a pop/rock trivia god), followed by the essential bits you need to learn the song:

✔ A run-down of the parts you need to know, not including those parts that are clones of other sections of the song.

✔ A breakdown of some of the chord progressions you need to play the song — the structure behind the sounds.

✔ When necessary, some info you need to navigate the sheet music (such as codas, repeats, and so on.)

Of course, you might already know a lot of this stuff, so feel free to skip it as you choose — unless you find the writing especially witty, entertaining, and eloquent (yeah, right). I suggest that you follow along in the music as I discuss the form and chord changes for each song. The best strategy is always to go through the song and find all the main sections and chords, then try working in all the licks and tricks. Approach the song one section at a time and then put them together in sequence. This strategy can give you greater understanding and enable you to play the song more quickly.

To follow the music and the performance notes, you need a basic understanding of scales and chords. If you're not a theory expert, don't worry. Just spend some time with *Music Theory For Dummies* (Wiley), and you'll be well prepared to use this book.

As you may expect, there are quite a few musical terms used in this book. Some of these may be unfamiliar to you, so I'd like to define a few for you:

- **Arpeggio** (playing the notes of a chord one at a time, rather than all together)

- **Bridge** (part of a song that is different from the verse and chorus; it provides variety and can serve to connect the other parts of a song)

- **Coda** (a section at the end of a song; sometimes the section is labeled with the word "coda")

- **Chorus** (the part of a song that is the same each time through; as a result, it is usually the best-known part of the song)

- **Chromatic** (moving by half steps; for example, C–B–Bb–A–Ab–G)

- **Hook** (in pop music, a familiar or catchy melody or lick)

- **Power chord** (notated with a 5 — C5, for example — this chord has no third, so it is neither major nor minor)

- **Progression** (a series of chords)

- **Resolution** (a progression that creates a sense of closure; 4–5–1 is a common resolution)

- **Slash chord** (a chord with a specific bass note listed to the right of the chord name — C/G, for example)

- **Suspended chord** (also known as a "sus chord," this is a chord where the 3rd has been raised to the 4th)

- **Verse** (the part of a song that tells the story; each verse has different lyrics; a song usually has two, three, or four of these)

Lastly, you may find the following chart helpful as you study the songs and performance notes. For each of the 12 major keys, it shows the basic chords built on that key's seven scale steps.

	1	2	3	4	5	6	7
Ab	Ab	Bbm	Cm	Db	Eb	Fm	Gdim
A	A	Bm	C#m	D	E	F#m	G#dim
Bb	Bb	Cm	Dm	Eb	F	Gm	Adim
B	B	C#m	D#m	E	F#	G#m	A#dim
C	C	Dm	Em	F	G	Am	Bdim
Db	Db	Ebm	Fm	Gb	Ab	Bbm	Cdim
D	D	Em	F#m	G	A	Bm	C#dim
Eb	Eb	Fm	Gm	Ab	Bb	Cm	Ddim
E	E	F#m	G#m	A	B	C#m	D#dim
F	F	Gm	Am	Bb	C	Dm	Edim
F#	F#	G#m	A#m	B	C#	D#m	E#dim
G	G	Am	Bm	C	D	Em	F#dim

Icons Used in This Book

In the margins of this book are several little icons that will help make your life easier:

 A reason to stop and review advice that can prevent damage to your fingers, ears, piano, or ego.

 Optional parts, like solos, that may be too challenging for many pianists, but are discussed anyway for the learned and/or ambitious "champion" players among you.

 Notes about specific musical concepts that are relevant but confusing to the layperson. Sometimes it's just something I notice that's especially cool to musicians!

 Suggestions to get through some of the difficult bits without tangling your fingers or your mind.

 Shortcuts and clues that, you guessed it, will save time.

Performance Notes

Against All Odds (Take a Look at Me Now)
(page 32)

This song was Phil Collins' first #1 hit in America as a solo artist and certainly not his last. From the fairly forgettable 1984 film of the same name, "Against All Odds" has been an enduring radio hit since its release.

Though the song sounds simple, its chords and structure are actually quite challenging. By playing through it slowly and feeling out the changes, you can get comfortable with the various suspended chords, slash chords, and other added notes that appear. That way, when you play it at the right tempo, you'll have some familiarity built up. If you're singing along, be prepared for the high notes; Collins has quite a range and uses it well.

Though the song is in the key of C major, it relates more to the relative key of A minor. Starting with two bars of Dm–G, the verse begins with a climbing pattern. Starting on a variation of Am, the song moves up through Bm, then C, then Dm, then F. The added notes on some of the chords are just dressing; pay attention to the root of the chord below to catch on to the fundamental progression and foundation. So a progression of Am7–Bm7–C(add2)–Dm7(add4)–F(add2) should be understood based on the root chords of Am–Bm–C–Dm–F. That way it's not as confusing to comprehend and play.

Always try to understand the chord progressions, instead of just reading the notes. The verse finishes out with a run of minor chords (Em–Am–Dm) leading to the G major chord at the end. Progressing in 5ths (for example, starting on E, down five notes to A, down five notes to D, down five notes to G, and so on) is a common technique used in pop chord progressions, moving them along toward eventual tension-release scenarios.

After the first verse, you repeat a verse that is exactly the same in structure. The only difference is the ending, which uses a Gsus to resolve to the G major chord, which then resolves to the C/G that begins the chorus. Collins rides the G bass line under the next chord (D7) before moving into the Am7–F–Dm7–Gsus progression that sets up the second half of the chorus. The second half uses the exact same chords except the Gsus resolves to G major, which then transitions back to the next verse. You then repeat a verse and chorus out, ending on the progression that was used on the intro and nicely resolving this tortured tale of lost love. Against all odds, you too can play this song — take a look at you now!

Alone (page 37)

Some songs work so well for a band that you'd never know the band didn't write them. "Alone," which was a huge hit for Heart, was written by the team of Billy Steinberg and Tom Kelly, the men responsible for such '80s hits as "Like a Virgin" and "Eternal Flame," recorded by Madonna and the Bangles, respectively. Steinberg and Kelly had actually recorded and released the song years earlier under their own band name, but it failed to catch fire. When they heard Heart was looking for a power ballad, they demoed the song and the rest is history. Interesting footnote: Kelly actually sang backups on the Heart version!

This song is in the key of D major, though it relates more to the relative key of B minor. The 4-bar intro uses the same chord progression as the first two lines of the verse which follow. The song begins on Bm, circling down through G and A. In D major, this would be m6–4–5, which is then followed by the transition chord A/G (5/4), a competent segue back to Bm. The second time around, after the A major chord you use an F♯7/A♯ — an even more effective transition chord. You can feel the tension of the build and the release to Bm. In the verse, you repeat this progression twice before moving into a descending pattern of G–D/F♯–G/E–D, which uses a descending bass line (G–F♯–E–D) underneath a G–D–G–D chord pattern. The progression repeats again, but instead of ending directly on D, use an Asus–A setup to resolve to the D major and prepare for the oncoming big pop chorus.

The chorus feels more like it's in the key of G major, which is very closely related to the root key of D major. You repeat the pattern Em–C–G–D three times before the tag line "How do I get you alone," which uses an ascending three chord pattern of G/B–C–D and repeats it a second time. At the end of the last bar of the chorus, a quick F♯m chord sets up the transition back to the Bm that begins the second verse. After the second verse and chorus, you move to the coda to repeat the chorus again and lead into the guitar solo. The guitar solo starts out on the chorus progression (Em–C–G–D) but changes up in the fifth bar to a descending progression of bass notes, which move from C–B–A–G–F♯–E–D–C before returning to the chorus line that runs B–C–D.

Be aware of patterns in the bass line so you can make sense of the chords as they move up or down. After a few repetitions of the chorus tag line, you end on the same chords that introduced the song, finishing on an unsettling Bm chord. Ending the song on the m6 chord leaves an unresolved feeling, highlighting the song's mood.

Back at One (page 42)

From his triple-platinum album of the same name, Brian McKnight's "Back at One" gave him the widest exposure of his career. The accompanying video portrayed a heart-wrenching scenario of a man on a crashing plane leaving a cell phone message for his wife (who avoids picking up the phone until it's too late).

The song is in the key of B major, which means maximum sharps and a lot of chords based on them. Take your time figuring out how to play through the chord changes and melody. If you're singing along with this one, you may want to stretch your vocal chords before attempting the high F at the end of the bridge. McKnight has some serious vocal chops, which is why he is a multi-platinum recording star. But fear not! By practicing quality material like the songs in this book, you can find your own style for hitting the high notes with McKnightly class.

The sheet music starts right on the verse with the root-based chord B(add2). From there, you follow the pattern 1–m6–4–m2 (B–G♯m–E–C♯m). Keep in mind that the added 2 notes and minor 7ths are dressing on the basic root chords. Between the C♯m7 and the B in the fifth bar, there is a quick transitional chord progression of D♯m7–E–F♯, which falls right along the numeric chord line (m3–4–5). After repeating the B(add2)–G♯m7, you step out with an atypical Amaj7 transitioning to the more formulaic E(add2)/G♯ behind it. The next chord is a slash chord that reads C♯/E♯.

Note that E♯ is the same as an F. Sometimes, theory gets so literal that it makes more sense to list it as E♯. You then repeat the Amaj7–E(add2)/G♯ progression again, but instead of that C♯/E♯ chord, you play the more formulaic C♯m7/F♯ as a terrific transition back to the B major root chord that begins the chorus.

The chorus follows an almost identical chord progression as the verse. You use an F♯sus transition chord between the G♯m7 and the E(add2) but other than that, they are virtually indistinguishable. This makes it a lot easier for you to learn the song! After the chorus finishes, you start back at one — pardon the pun — with the root B chord that begins the second verse, which then is followed by another chorus. That second chorus winds to a close on that B–G♯m–E–C♯m progression, though this time the ending transitions to a bridge. You enter the bridge with the C♯m7/F♯ transition to an E major chord, the 4 chord in the key of B major. You use the descending E–B/D♯ twice before jumping to the very dramatic G♯ variations that follow. This is a pretty chord change that also functions as a great transition to the C♯m7 that follows.

The next progression falls along the scale chords: the C♯m7–D♯m7–G♯m7–C♯m7 = m2–m3–m6–m2 in the root key. McKnight ends the bridge with an upward motion, raising the bass on the C♯m7 to F♯ and continuing upward with the Dm7/G–G/B that follows. Of course, you'll be passed out from singing the melody note so you may not notice!

When the bridge ends, the key transposes a half step higher to C major. You repeat a chorus in the new key, ending on the new root chord (C major). Notice how the fundamental chord structure works the same in the new key and compare it to the old one for added measure. The outro is a lovely progression based on 4–m6–m2–m2/5 and ending on a classy Amaj9 chord.

Candle in the Wind *(page 47)*

Written as a tribute to the late Marilyn Monroe (birth name Norma Jean), this is one of Elton John's bestselling songs in his huge catalog of hits. The "candle in the wind" represents a life snuffed out too soon, so it was appropriate that Elton re-recorded it in 1997 in honor of the passing of Princess Diana with a new chorus, "good-bye, English rose." It became the biggest selling single in history.

The song is in the key of E major and virtually the entire song is made up of chords from that scale — a very helpful fact to be aware of as you play. The intro starts on the 5 chord (B) before descending from A–A/G♯–F♯m7–E. Make use of a quick E–Esus–E to transition to the B and then the B7, setting up the 5–1 release back to the root chord of E major. The verse chords are simple to play through and don't change too fast, giving you ample time to react to the changes. Notice the A–D/A–A progressions, which are just mini–resolutions to establish a chord — in this case, A major. The A at the end of the verse transitions to the B major chord that begins the chorus. The chorus chords are also simple, sticking to the 1–4–5–m6 chords of the scale. At the end, you transition down from A–A/G♯–F♯m7–E much like you did before the first verse. You play another verse and chorus and then enter a third verse and final chorus, repeating the last line for maximum effect. You ends with the trademark A–A/G♯–F♯m7–E transition that you played earlier in this song, ending on the root E major chord, the ultimate resolution.

Changes *(page 54)*

Singer-songwriter David Bowie didn't originally think "Changes" would be much of a hit, but what started out as a throwaway album cut morphed into one of his best-known classics and fan favorites. Keyboardist Rick Wakeman (from Yes) played piano on the track, and Bowie himself handled the saxophone work at the end of the song.

The song is in the key of C major, which means the scale chords are very basic: C–Dm–Em–F–G–Am–Bdim (1–m2–m3–4–5–m6–dim7). Bowie starts with an ascending chromatic chord progression in the intro, moving from C–D♭–D–E♭ to the F that begins the eighth-note staccato chord pounding. Bowie moves from D to F twice before resolving to the root C major chord that begins the verse. That D–F–C chord pattern is a version of the very common 2–5–1 resolution. The verse sticks mainly with scale chords, moving along a 1–m3–4–5 pattern twice. After the second time, Bowie follows with a chord pattern of C–Dm7–Em7–E♭m7–Dm7. Notice how he rises to the Em7 then falls chromatically back to the Dm7 chord, which then resolves up to the G and back down to C major — another 2–5–1 resolution. He repeats the line and starts into the chorus with 5–4–1 resolution (G7–F–C) beneath the famous "ch–ch–ch–ch–changes" lyric.

The chorus is a descending chord progression beginning on the root chord (C major) and moving down along the bass line C–B–A–G–F–E–D and then to G to resolve back to the root again. The next time he reaches the D major chord at the bottom of the progression, Bowie tags each word of the lyrics with individual chords. Under "Time may change me" you play Am–G–B♭–F and then use the F to start the descending chord pattern to end on the root chord of C major. You then repeat part of the intro followed by a second verse and chorus musically identical to the first ones. Out of the C major that ends the second chorus, you go into the bridge via the progression C–Dm7–Em7–F (1–m2–m3–4). The bridge is really based on three chords — the C, F, and G (1, 4, and 5). Bowie uses the staccato eighth-note chords in the right hand through the bridge to give a strong sense of motion.

The bridge leads right into the descending chord progression of the chorus and repeats it out. After the last line of the chorus, Bowie adds a little instrumental section that first moves up to the Em7 chord and then moves down chromatically (E–E♭–D–D♭–C) to end on the root chord of C major with full resolution. This song was meant to be played on piano, so have fun with it!

Clocks *(page 60)*

Legend has it that this mega-selling song was not going to make it onto Coldplay's *Rush of Blood to the Head* record until a friend heard the demo and convinced the band to do whatever it took to record it. Luckily they did, because the song beat out Outkast and Beyonce for the 2003 GRAMMY® for Record Of The Year, showing that sensitive English piano players can still make the magic happen.

This song is in the key of E♭ major. The main piano lick is a three-note, descending arpeggio that runs along the chord pattern listed. Starting on E♭/G, which is the root chord with its 3rd as the bass, the next chord is a m5 chord (B♭m) over F, moving to a basic Fm, which is the m2 chord. Then it moves to a straighter section, without the slash chord bass notes, moving from an E♭ major chord to B♭m. The Fm then provides an easy resolution to the E♭ major chord that starts the verse.

Luckily, the verse just repeats these three chords, making it easy to play all the way through the first ending. In that ending, instead of Fm you substitute an A♭6 chord. When you play them, you'll see these chords aren't that different.

After repeating a second verse and chorus, the second ending leads to the bridge. Starting with a pretty G♭maj7 chord and leading through a D♭ to A♭ change, you repeat this three times, and on the third time you return to the G♭maj7 for four bars. You then have an exact repeat of the instrumental intro section and its descending triplets.

The sheet music now jumps back a page for a repeating chorus before skipping ahead to the coda. The pattern here is similar to the intro, with descending triplet arpeggios over a repetitive eighth-note bass. The only difference is the A♭maj7 chord (the major 4) which gives a nice variety to the pattern.

Jumping now to the coda on the last page, you play a variation on the chorus as lead singer Chris Martin wishes he could go home, perhaps much like Dorothy in the Wizard of Oz, but without the pretty shoes. In any case, you end on the repeating arpeggios that make up the staple riff of this song and either fade out or end on the root chord. This is a pretty song. The triplets definitely exercise your right hand and enhance your ability to arpeggiate chords.

Come Sail Away (page 66)

The song "Come Sail Away" was huge for Styx, adding to their vast '70s classic rock canon. It's imagery of starships and descending angels caught on with a wide variety of people and was one of their biggest hits. The intro is a recognizable piece of music that lets listeners know they're about to embark on a lengthy synth-drenched prog rock journey on an open course for the virgin sea.

The song is in the key of C major and uses only the chords from the scale. You play the majority of these chords on the white keys, simplifying your practice a good bit. Also, the song doesn't follow a normal verse-chorus structure, so be prepared for a variety of sections, beginning with the intro.

The intro works off a sixteenth-note bass pattern played under an eighth-note right hand pattern. Practice each of these separately before playing them together so you can learn the intro more quickly. The pattern of the chord structure under the intro is 1–m2–m3–m2–1 as a setup to the 5 chord (G) to resolve back to the root chord, C major. The verse follows a descending pattern that follows the bass line downward, C–B–A–G–F, before moving to the G to resolve to C again. That 4–5–1 resolution (F–G–C) is very common in pop music. The line is repeated twice and then you move to a kind of pre-chorus section which uses Am–G–Am–G to set up the descending pattern that ends the section with "to carry on." You then repeat the intro verbatim and launch into another verse. This verse and the subsequent prechorus lead to the repeat of the "carry on" ending, which this time takes you into the Big Rock Section, which was mandatory in classic '70s FM rock.

In this section, you play a C–F–G pattern over a steady C bass note. Play these chords loud and with feeling. This chord pattern repeats through the next section that features the title "Come Sail Away" repeated over and over. The one chord that is outside of the scale chords comes at the very end of the page when they land on an A♭. In the recorded version it is a very mystical A♭, full of synthesizers and guitars but I'm sure you'll do it justice with whatever keyboard you're on! After you're done being mystical, jump right back into the rock section and gear up to sing "Come sail away" again and again. If you have a crowd of friends, everyone can sing along and you can really rock it out. But if you're alone, don't hesitate to belt this one out at top volume. You'll feel better, even if your neighbors don't!

Don't Know Much (page 72)

One of the best-known duets in modern pop, the pairing of Linda Ronstadt and Aaron Neville produced a string of hits including their biggest hit "Don't Know Much." Between Ronstadt's clear and wide range and Neville's quavering falsetto, the pair made a vocal match that scored well with audiences worldwide. This song was actually co-written by the classic team of Barry Mann and Cynthia Weil along with collaborator Tom Snow and it shows all the hallmarks of classic songwriting and composition.

This song is in the key of C major and it begins with two repetitions of an F–C resolution that uses the 4–5–1 chords (F–G–C) over a climbing F–A–B–C bassline. Whereas the verse sticks mainly to the chords of the C major scale, the bridge uses some unorthodox but nicely arranged chording before the song switches key midway to E♭ major.

The verse is built on the chords of the C major scale. The slash chords allow for movement in the bass that enhances the progression. For instance, the C–F–G of the first line has a lot more movement as C–C/E–F/A–G/B. The chorus begins on the m6 (Am) and runs Am–F–G–Em–F, which is m6–4–5–m3–4 in the C major scale. The last line is one big resolution to C that moves from F/A–G/B–C–F–G–Csus–C. All that motion works to build tension before setting up the release to the root chord. After this, you repeat a verse and chorus, again ending on the root chord of C major. From here you move into the bridge, which starts on A minor.

You transition from C to Am7 via a G/B chord that drops you into the bridge. The progression Am–D–G would be a 2–5–1 resolution in G, which makes the following root chord (Cmaj7) sound like a 4 chord. However, the F–F/G–C that follows reestablishes the root with its 4–4/5–1 resolution. The next line gets very interesting as it sets up the key change to E♭ major. The C major chord becomes a Cm7, which is the relative minor of E♭ major.

Although you're still in the key of C major, you want to understand how these chords relate to the upcoming key change. In fact, if compared to the key of E♭ major, the Cm7–E♭/F–B♭maj9–E♭maj9 progression becomes the m6–1/2–5–1. Follow that with the A♭–E♭/G–Fm7–E♭/G that sets up the A♭/B♭ combos, which in turn set up the resolution into the new chord change. In E♭ major, A♭/B♭ is a 4/5 chord, one of the most common setups for resolution. A quick B♭/D chord transitions into the actual E♭ major chord that begins the last verse in the new key. Compare the pattern of chords with previous verses: The numerical progression remains the same even though the chords themselves are different.

You wind down the repeated chorus lines on a lingering resolution of E♭sus to a final E♭(add2), a pretty ending to a pretty song. By examining the similarities in chord patterns before and after the key change, you'll be better able to understand the structure and foundation of the song.

Don't Know Why *(page 78)*

Consider this song a monster debut for Norah Jones. At the 2003 GRAMMY Awards, Jones won all five awards she was nominated for, including Best New Artist, Record Of The Year, and Song Of The Year! Quite an amazing run for a mellow, jazzy chanteuse from the Big Apple. The song was actually written by Jones' guitar player Jesse Harris, who had previously recorded it with his own band. At the tender age of 21, Jones recorded her album version in just one take.

This "moderately slow" song is in the key of B♭ major, so be on the lookout for the chords of that scale. One thing you see is the use of C major and D major chords rather than the more scale-friendly C minor and D minor chord. They're used in ways that are more transitional, usually to initiate a resolution to another chord. The intro starts on the root (B♭) before moving to the 4 (E♭) and then using a D major chord to move to Gm7, setting up the resolution Gm–C–F–B♭ (m6–2–5–1) into the verse. The verse starts on the root (B♭) as well and follows the intro chords with the exception of the D+ chord, which adds to its transitory nature between E♭ and Gm. The augmented fifth note of the D chord (B♭) is the fifth note of the E♭ before it and the minor third of the Gm after it. Instead of a true chorus, Jones repeats the "Don't know why" line multiple times during the verse. When she repeats that line, she transitions out with an F7sus–B♭–F7sus–B♭maj7 that nicely sets up the second verse.

At the end of that verse on the second page, you resolve to the root B♭ major chord, after which you move to a second section. That second section uses the progression Gm7–C7–F7 (m6–2–5) twice before using the second F7 to begin a descending chord progression that follows the bass line, F–E♭–D–C–B♭, leading you into the next verse. This transition is pretty and the last chord (F/C) works well because it is a 5/2 chord, another variant of the 2–5–1 resolution you've seen so often.

After that comes a verse and then a repeat of that second section, followed by an instrumental verse. Jones then sings a verse featuring the title line ("Don't know why") before ending with the C7–F7–B♭ (2–5–1) resolve to the root chord. This beautiful song is fairly easy to play due to its repetitive nature.

Dreamer (page 84)

A staple on rock radio in the '70s and '80s, England's Supertramp scored a string of hits based around electric piano and lush harmonies. The song "Dreamer" comes from the 1974 *Crime of the Century* album, which also spawned the hit "Bloody Well Right." "Dreamer" was Supertramp's first UK Top 20 hit and put them on the map in the world of rock 'n' roll.

The song is in the key of D major and it begins with a repetitive eighth-note keyboard riff built on the D major chord. When the chorus kicks in with the title lyric "Dreamer," the D then rotates through an A7sus–A7 setup to return to D. The second time the A7 leads to a C–Fmaj7 change into a G–D resolution. The C and F chords aren't from the D major scale but they work well setting up the G that resolves back to D. This whole six-bar section is repeated and then the F–G change is used twice to set up the half step rise to A♭.

This section, with the unexpected use of A♭ and B♭, doesn't really relate to the key of D major, but it works in context with itself. You repeat a four-bar chord pattern that is based on A♭–B♭–Gm–C. At the end you repeat the Gm–C again and transition right back to the D major chord that begins the chorus. You repeat these two sections, and at the end the Gm–C leads you into an instrumental part with an insistent eighth-note keyboard part that pumps a series of right hand chords across a sparse bass line. The main chords given are C–B♭/C, but the changes can be challenging, so you may need to practice this part carefully. As you keep rotating the C and B♭/C chords, lyrics come in and lead a call-and-answer section. At some point the chord combination switches to C–Gm7/C, which is very similar to the B♭/C you played before. At the bottom of the eighth page, the keyboards begin a back-and-forth pattern of C–F/C, which soon drops to a B♭–C/B♭ pattern. This leads to a B♭maj7 chord, which resolves back up to the D major chord.

Back in the root key of D, you're ready to go into the chorus. You play through to the end of this section, which repeats Fmaj7–G twice before stopping on the G to fade out under the little melody on the bells. There is an "optional ending" here if you really need to wind down on the bell solo, but feel free to fade out!

Drops of Jupiter (Tell Me) (page 95)

Train had a minor hit off their debut album with the song "Meet Virginia," but it was this monster hit from their sophomore record (also called *Drops of Jupiter*) that established the band as chart-topping hit makers. The song won two GRAMMY Awards and, accordingly, sold a lot of records. The strings were arranged by Paul Buckmaster, who had become famous arranging for the Rolling Stones, Elton John, and David Bowie. Legendary keyboardist Chuck Leavell played the piano parts, and singer Pat Monahan sealed the deal with his impassioned vocal performance.

The song is in the key of C major and sticks closely to the scale chords. The intro is a basic 1–5–4 progression (C–G–F) that resolves to the C major chord that begins the verse. The verse works on that same chord progression (C–G–F) three times through, making it simple to learn and play. The chorus, which begins with the words "Tell me," moves along the progression G–D–F–C, using slash chords for transitions like the G–G/A–D pattern or the D–C/E–F that follows. Those transitional chords help move the song around its structural foundation. That F chord releases to C to set up the return to the G major chord that begins the chorus. The G moves again from G–G/A–D but then makes the D major into a D minor chord, which sets up the Dm–C/E–F progression that follows. That F resolves to the root chord of C major, beginning the instrumental section you played in the introduction.

After the intro section, you repeat a second verse and chorus, and again wind up resolving to C after the chorus. That in turn leads into the bridge, which is mainly comprised of C, G, and F chords or variations thereof. Starting with two rotations of C–G–F, the band winds up with an F–G–C resolution, using the C to transition to B♭ and then F. (***Note:*** The B♭ chord works more because of it's relation to the F rather than to the C. In the key of F major, B♭ and C would be the 4 and 5 chords, making it a reliable chord change.) But that F gives you a place to transition up a step to the G major chord that begins the last chorus.

After repeating the chorus, you're lead out to the coda where you get to sing a big "na na na na" over a repeating C–G–F (1–5–4) progression. This progression is varied only at the very end, where the G moves to a B♭–C/B♭–B♭ setup to end on the F chord. This setup and resolution reinforce the feeling of being in the key of F major even though you are still in C. (In reference to F, the B♭–C/B♭ would be the 4–5/4 change to resolve to 1.) Train may have tricked your ears a bit and left you stranded on the 4 chord (F), but it's better than being left on Jupiter!

Fallin' *(page 104)*

A discovery of the legendary Clive Davis, Alicia Keys was only 20 when she set the R&B world on fire with this song, her first single. The album it came from went on to sell over 10 million copies and is certified diamond, which is 10X platinum. "Fallin'" won the 2001 GRAMMY Awards for Song Of The Year, Best Female R&B Vocal Performance, and Best R&B Song, and Keys also won awards for Best New Artist and Best R&B Album, a staggering feat for a new artist.

This song has a 12/8 time signature, which lends it a kind of waltz feel that supports the gentle eighth-note arpeggios that appear throughout the song. Though the song is in the key of G major, it relates more to the relative key of E minor. The song begins on a back-and-forth progression of Em–Bm and doesn't deviate from this formula for the entire song.

Because this song has a fair amount of repetition, it tests your ability to keep an arpeggio moving while you sing over the top of it. Whether you're playing the melody or singing it, play the arpeggio with the left hand and the sparse chording and melody with the right hand. You have ample room to improvise on the chords, so feel free to elaborate or embellish the song to create your own version.

Good Vibrations *(page 111)*

The California sun soaked into Brian Wilson's brain to give him the inspiration for the exuberant "Good Vibrations." With a simple organ foundation, the song begins its classic tale of a guy attracted to a girl who gives him the aforementioned good vibes. The song's overall production is definitely rooted in Phil Spector's "Wall of Sound," replete with hugely reverberated harmonies, tambourine hits, and a jangly piano in the breakdown. Released in 1966, it was the most expensive pop song ever produced! The strange noise you hear behind the chorus is an instrument called a *theramin*, which has been used to provide these kinds of spacey effects for *Star Trek* and other TV shows and movies.

This song isn't structured in your typical verse-chorus-verse setup, showing Wilson's creativity in constructing his own style. You see many key changes and a complete dynamic breakdown in the middle from which you build the song back up for its climactic ending. Wilson is known for his vocal arrangements and this song is no exception; indeed, the Beach Boys' tight, post-barbershop vocalizing was exceptional in its day and remains so today. Whatever aspect of the song you focus on — structure, performance, arrangement, instrumentation — you can discover a lot about the genius involved in this song while having fun with the performance. Brother Carl Wilson sang lead on this song, which was the Beach Boys last #1 song until the fluffy "Kokomo," 22 years later. At this writing, that is the longest time between #1 hits for any recorded act!

This song changes keys numerous times throughout, so here's the scoop on how that affects the overall structure as well as the chords that are used. The song begins in the key of F major, and Wilson starts the verse in the relative D minor using a descending chord pattern. Wilson uses an A major chord as a turnaround to the C7 that resolves to the chorus, which starts in F major. The chorus employs a 1–4 chord combination (F7–B♭/F), riding the root (F) underneath. Wilson then moves that pattern a whole step up to G for four bars and then another whole step to A for another 4 bars. This A then proceeds to resolve back to Dm for the next verse.

After the second verse, the key changes to D major. Changing keys from D minor to D major mid-song is a neat twist, and Wilson makes it work. The D major section has a lot of slash chords. He switches these up throughout, so you may want to take this section slow to feel the movement of the bass note against the right-hand chords.

For the next section, Wilson goes one step further with the next transition to E major. In E major, Wilson uses a repeating 1–2–5 chord pattern (E–F♯m–B7) until he introduces a fourth key change, to A major, followed by a descending key change to G major, then another one back to F major. Just for kicks, Wilson ends the song with one more key change to C major, a nice resolution from F.

Hard to Say I'm Sorry (page 120)

"Hard to Say I'm Sorry" is one of Chicago's biggest '80s hits. Any song that enables men to communicate their feelings to women is bound to do well, and as women know, some men have a lot to be sorry for! The song intro nicely foreshadows the structure and melody of the pre-chorus, setting up vocalist/songwriter Peter Cetera's classic opening line "Everybody needs a little time away." You find some great chords in this song with lots of suspended chords and a lot of movement through the progressions.

The band holds back, not kicking in fully until the second verse, giving the song a nice chance to build its energy so it can deliver maximum emotional impact. Interestingly, the band builds on a repeating pre-chorus as an intro to the solo, which is a massive, building affair full of guitars and strings and an inexplicable rock section that enters just past the four-minute mark. This turning point transforms a sensitive wedding-worthy love song into an ELO-style horns and synths workout. It's as if two completely separate songs were magically mashed together, just in case you needed to rock out after your nuptials. If you're playing this song on piano alone, you may not feel the pure excitement of a massive horn section pumping you along, but fear not! Your imagination is about to get a workout, which is never a bad idea. Then perhaps you can contemplate how love songs vary in shades of bombast and add your own '80s-inspired flourishes.

The song is in the key of E major but toward the end it jumps a step and a half to G major. Take your time feeling out the bass notes in the slash chords peppered throughout to get a grasp on the movement of the bass line. By playing different bass notes against the chords, Cetera moves intricately through his changes, setting up resolutions and transitions that are much deeper than your average three-chord pop songs.

The intro foreshadows the chorus and leads into a fairly straightforward verse. Take the chorus slow as you feel out the changes; it may take you time to get comfortable with how fast Cetera's chord transitions change. In this song, he uses a lot of descending bass lines, so be sure to look for that pattern as you practice the song. After you're familiar with how the song works, it will be much easier to play up to speed. Then it won't be so hard to say you're sorry!

Have I Told You Lately *(page 126)*

This simple love song, penned by none other than Van Morrison, has become a staple at weddings due to its universal themes of devotion, faith, and love. This is one of the easier songs to play in this book because it is a straight 4/4 ballad with no tricky changes or chords. As the saying goes, sometimes less is more and in this case, a lot more. It's harder than it seems to write a simple song, and this one benefits from the ubiquitous "you" in the title, leaving room for any "you" that you want to express your love to sooner than later.

You can find a variety of recordings of this classic to practice with. Rod Stewart's husky voice has been successful on a wide variety of musical styles, from the '60s roots rock of the Faces through his '70s disco-pop, then his '80s synth-rock and, most recently, the classic standards that have truly rejuvenated his career. Though most people are familiar with this song through Stewart, Morrison's tender original version is a beauty and shouldn't be overlooked.

The song is in the key of B♭ and follows some simple patterns. Interestingly, this song doesn't have a traditional chorus; rather, the first line of the verse is the title of the song and it works very well. The verse has an upward motion, starting on the 1 chord (B♭) and moving towards the 4 chord (E♭) with the classic 4/5 setup (in this case E♭/F) to resolve back to the 1. The second section has a downward motion, moving from the 4 chord (E♭bmaj7) back down to the root. In the bridge, the song returns to that pretty 4 chord (E♭maj7), teasing its way downward to the minor 2 chord (Dm7) to set up that 4/5 chord (E♭/F) that so nicely resolves to the 1 for the last verse. That 2–5–1 resolution is very common, and this won't be the last time you see or hear it. This song plays it very safe, never leaving the scale of the key it's in, and so its changes are easy to follow and play. And won't you be happy knowing how much Rod and Van love you!

Hello *(page 131)*

Starting with a simple minor key chord progression, Lionel Richie's song of unrequited love has stood the test of time since hitting #1 on the charts. According to legend, Richie left this song off his first post-Commodores solo album, but included it on his second *(Can't Slow Down)* at the insistence of his wife. Of course, that second album won the 1984 GRAMMY for Album Of The Year and became the biggest selling album in the history of Motown Records — no small feat, considering the label's hefty catalog!

Much has been made of the video for this song, featuring a smitten Richie longing for a blind student in his sculpture class. But put the creepy imagery from the video out of your mind; there are some lovely chord changes in the song's chorus, making great use of suspended chords to support the lyrics and Richie's eventual profession of "I love you." Add a simply structured guitar solo (which Richie seems fond of in his songs) and the most basic of drumming and drum fills and you've got a classic on your hands.

A unique feature of this song is its major key chorus, which contrasts so nicely with the minor key verse. On the verse, you simply repeat the descending pattern of m6–5–4 (Am–G–F) over and over, until you make use of a bright A major chord to transition to the Dm of the chorus. Though the song is in C major, that A major chord steps out of the scale a bit to provide a setup for the resolution to the chorus, and it works amazingly well.

When you reach the chorus, work through the chords slowly. You play some slash chords and an ascending bass line, which may take time to get comfortable with. The chorus is very pretty and the chord changes are smooth and powerful. You end the chorus on an E major chord, which sets up the resolution back to the Am of the verse. Richie expertly brings the song to a close on an A major chord, giving a final feeling of resolution that nicely matches the culmination of the story line.

Hey Jude (page 134)

Written by Paul McCartney, the song's original title was "Hey Jules," which was meant to console John Lennon's son Julian when his parents were divorcing. The name was changed to Jude with a little inspiration from the character named Jud in the musical *Oklahoma*. At over seven minutes in length, the song was an unlikely hit, but fans responded (it was The Beatles, after all), and the full version got a lot of airplay. The song was recorded over a period of two days and features a 26-piece orchestra to bolster the impact of the sing-along refrain (you know, the "na, na, na, na-na-na-na" part). Actually, the repeating fadeout comprises more than half the length of the song! Take that, "Freebird."

The song is in the key of F major and for the most part sticks to the chords of the F major scale. The song's two main sections are the verse, which includes the title, and the second part, which is neither a chorus or bridge, but a separate secondary section. On the verse, you start in the root chord of F major and then go to the 5 chord (C major). To transition back from that C, McCartney uses a little C7–C7sus–C7 pattern. The sus chord resolves the C7 back to itself, which then sets up the resolution back to the root chord of F major. This is a classic double resolution, an important tool in setting up chord transitions for maximum impact.

The root changes of the verse are F–C–F–B♭–F–C–F. Numerically, this is simply 1–5–1–4–1–5–1, using the most basic of pop music chord changes. Indeed, the 4 and 5 chords are the most common chords used in conjunction with the 1 chord; you can find thousands of hit songs that solely rely on the 1–4–5 chords, and this one is no exception.

On the second page, you repeat the verse the same as before and then go into the second section. To transition out of the verse, McCartney takes the root F and adds a minor 7 (F7) to set up the change to the 4 chord (B♭). You then begin a descending chord pattern back to the F that involves some slash chords.

Notice the bass line descending along the F major scale: B♭–A–G–F–E and then C before returning to F. The chords on top work with those notes and accentuate their descent. B♭ becomes B♭/A, Gm7 becomes Gm7/F and C7/E becomes C7 which sets up the 5–1 resolution back to the root chord of F major. This is repeated again the exact same way, after which the F becomes an F7 to transition to the C7 that ends the section. That C7 — a 5 chord with an added dominant 7 — is a powerful transition back to the root chord that restarts the verse.

You play through the last sections again before ending on the F major chord beneath the "better, better, better" line. That kicks off the final fadeout with a scream — prepare your neighbors so they don't call the cops on you! The finale is simple, just a repeating progression of three major chords: F–E♭–B♭ over and over again with the "na, na, na, na-na-na-na" vocal repeating like a mantra. On record, the fadeout takes about four minutes, though you're not bound by law to repeat it that long. Without the orchestra singing along, it may seem a bit anticlimactic. It's great for sing-alongs at parties, though!

I Believe I Can Fly (page 138)

Of all the things R. Kelly believes he can do, flying is probably the most legal. Written for the half-animated movie *Space Jam*, this song won three GRAMMY Awards in 1997, showing a side of Kelly that fans of "Feelin' on Yo Booty" might have never thought possible. However, the song has become a modern standard of sorts and an anthem of inspiration.

The song is in the key of C major, but you use some chords in the mix that are atypical and deserve some close scrutiny. Starting with a C(add9)/G (which is just like a C chord, but with an added 2 note), you change back and forth with a very dramatic Dm7♭5 that is also set over G. The bass remains constant on the 5 (G) to build up tension that releases to the root chord (C major) that starts the verse. In the verse, you alternate between a straight C major chord and that Dm7♭5, keeping the bass constant on the root note of C. You repeat that four times before moving through a transitory E7♯5, which works really well to take you to the Am7 that starts the pre-chorus.

A *pre-chorus* works as a transitional buildup between the verse and the chorus, and this one does a nice job. From the Am7, notice the descending bass line that moves from A–A♭–G to set up the return to the C that starts the chorus. The chords of the pre-chorus include that same dramatic Dm7♭5, though here it is played over the A♭. So far, that is the third bass note that has been used to augment this same chord (G in the intro and C in the verse are the other two). From that Dm7♭5/A♭ chord, you descend to the C/G and then the Dm7/G to set up the return to the root. You can feel the build and release to that C major chord, which is the purpose of the change.

The chorus is a fairly straightforward 1–m6–m2–5 rotation, though instead of a straight 5 chord, Kelly uses a Dm7/G and then a quick G♯dim7 to move to the m6 (Am7) that follows. Chords like the G♯dim7 are meant to build pure tension for the release of the change, and when you play it, you feel and hear the setup. Watch the movement in the bass line that follows: A–A♭–G–A♭–A–G, moving between A and G to set up the release back to the C of the verse. The chords are familiar throughout, using an Am7, followed by the memorable Dm7♭5 over the A♭ bass, then a C/G before moving right back to that Dm7♭5/A♭ chord and the Am7, a little circle of chords. After the Am7, you play a very pretty Fmaj7/G, which will resolve back to the root C major chord of the verse.

After a second repetition of verse and chorus, Kelly takes you to that Am7 and then uses it to transition to the Dm7 that begins the bridge. You start out the bridge with an ascending pattern of Dm7–C/E–Fmaj7/G before a serious key change takes effect, moving up a half step into the key of D♭ major. The relative minor key is B♭m, which is why you start on a B♭m7 chord. The following E♭m7♭5 chord is the same as the Dm7♭5 chord — it's just a half step up because of the key change. The chords themselves are fundamentally the same even though the key has changed. This key change can seen confusing until you realize all the similarities and patterns beneath the music.

Notice the descending bass note pattern in this section (B♭–A–A♭) and that the chord changes (B♭m7–E♭m7♭5–D♭–E♭m7) move in a very tight pattern before resolving to the D♭ major that is now the root key of the song. As this final chorus plays out, the changes are identical to earlier choruses even though you're a half step up in key. Comparing the two choruses can help you understand the song better and get a grip on the concept that numerical patterns in scales don't change even when the key changes. But because the piano is an uneven landscape, the chords look a lot different from key to key. Relax and trust your ears; they will not lead you astray.

(Everything I Do) I Do It for You *(page 144)*

Although Bryan Adams was known as a rocker with hits such as "Cuts Like a Knife" and "Summer of '69," this Canadian also scored big hits with ballads. "Everything I Do" is no exception. Featured in the Kevin Costner movie *Robin Hood: Prince of Thieves*, the song became one of the most successful singles of all time, staying at #1 in the United States for 7 weeks and in the United Kingdom for 16 weeks! The song went to #1 in 30 countries and won a GRAMMY in 1992, no small feat even for an established songwriter and artist like Adams. The song was produced by legendary rock producer Mutt Lange, who has had the magic touch with bands such as Def Leppard, AC/DC, and The Cars (not to mention wife Shania Twain). It has become a modern Adult Contemporary staple, and if you play it for your loved one, they will either be thrilled or they will run out of the room screaming. Either way, it's nice to evoke an emotional reaction!

The song is in the key of D♭ major, which involves using a lot of black keys in the chords. If you really want the easy way out, use the guitar version on top, which is in the much more manageable key of C major. However, this provides only the chord chart and not any of the staff notation, which remains in D♭.

The intro of the song is a four-bar pattern of D♭–A♭sus/D♭–G♭/D♭–A♭sus/D♭. Note that the bass remains the same — the root note of D♭. The chord pattern (D♭–A♭–G♭–A♭) is based on 1–5–4–5, to set up the resolution to the root 1 chord (D♭) that begins the verse. The chords that follow the D♭ (D♭sus–A♭/D♭) work to transition to the G♭ that follows, a 1–4 (D♭–G♭) movement. The next bar features variations on the 5 chord (A♭) before returning to D♭. You repeat the pattern, but in the last bar Adams uses a 1/5–5 (D♭/A♭–A♭) setup to the chorus. The chorus begins on the m2 (E♭m) and moves back and forth between E♭m and the root D♭, then jumps to the 5 (A♭sus) and back to 1 for the title line "Everything I do, I do it for you." This 1–5–1 resolution is common, take note of it whenever it appears.

After the chorus, you repeat a second verse and chorus and wind up on the D♭ major chord again. From here you enter the bridge by moving to a C♭ chord. In case you're not a music theory buff, a C♭ chord is, for all practical purposes, a B chord. These two chords use the same notes on the keyboard; they have two different names because they relate slightly differently to other chords. You move from C♭ to F♭ (B–E) and then C♭–G♭ before winding up back on the root D♭ major chord. From there, you move to an A♭–E♭–A♭ ending that holds the A♭ through a sus change to drop it back to G♭ for the instrumental part. You move from G♭–D♭ twice before beginning the chorus on E♭m but it progresses differently than before. From E♭m you move to A♭ (a m2–5 change) twice and then back to D♭–A♭, then G♭–G♭m to set up the D♭/A♭–A♭sus–A♭ that resolves to the final D♭ major chord through the 4 (G♭).

So that whole progression was based on D♭–A♭–G♭–G♭m–D♭/A♭–A♭–G♭–D♭, which is 1–5–4–m4–1/5–5–4–1. You set it up with a 1–5–4 transition with a m4 to a mini-resolution to the 5, which then walks down the final resolution of 5–4–1. Looking at the chords numerically helps you to see the flow of the patterns and progressions in a new light.

I Don't Want to Wait (page 154)

"I Don't Want to Wait" (also known as the theme to "Dawson's Creek"), was the second hit from Paula Cole's sophomore album *This Fire*, which garnered seven GRAMMY nominations in 1998 and put Cole on the musical map in a big way. This heartfelt song deals with the uncertainties of love and life as one tries to avoid future regrets and remorse. Though this is ultimately a futile quest, Cole's song touches on the emotions we all feel as we attempt to be sure and secure in our paths.

This pretty song introduces you to some neat variations of major and minor chords. The intro to the song is in the key of C major and has a twice-repeating descending bass line that runs F–E–D–C beneath a Gsus2 chord. The verse switches to the key of G major and you play a G(add2) chord, a variation of the Gsus2 chord. (The difference is that you're playing the 3 along with the 2, rather than playing the 2 instead of the 3. Subtle, yes, but it works for Cole and for the listener.) For the first part of the verse, there are only two chords: the aforementioned G(add2) juxtaposed with a C6/9. However, the two chords are notated very similarly, so don't worry about the labels; just focus on your fingers.

From the second G(add2) of the verse, you change to a descending chord pattern of Em7–D–Cmaj9, then do it a second time with slight variations (D6 instead of a straight D major, C(add9) instead of a Cmaj9). These differences are subtle and shouldn't distract from the underlying E–D–C descent. The 4 chord (C major) sets up the resolution back to the G(add2) that begins the chorus with its big recognizable hook.

The chorus works on a descending chord pattern that follows along the bass line, running G–F♯–E–D–C–B–A right along the G major scale, then turning around on a D to resolve back to the root chord — the ever-popular 5–1 resolution. Cole dresses up her chords with added 4ths, 11ths and 9ths, but the foundation is really simple. If you took away the additions, it could just as easily go G–D/F♯–Em–D–C–G/B–D/A–D. Just be aware of the foundation so that you understand the context of the different chord variations.

After the chorus, you repeat the intro chords of G(add2) and C6/9 before repeating the verse and chorus verbatim. The very last chord of the second chorus (Dsus/A) leads into the bridge. Notice that the bridge has a key change back to C major, even though it begins with a G7(add4) chord. Cole moves through some very dressed-up chords — Am9♭13, B♭(add2), Fsus, and C(add9). You can see the foundation of these chords by looking at them as G–Am–B♭–F–C, which can help you to make sense of the fundamental underlying progression before you add the extra notes. To use an analogy, understanding the basic chords before the extra notes are added is like knowing the cake recipe before adding the frosting. The bridge repeats this chord pattern before leading to the intro section with the Gsus2 chord played over a descending bass line of F–E–D–C. Following that, you switch back to the key of G major and repeat the chorus out, finishing with the G(add2) to C6/9 that you played earlier in the song.

I Will Remember You *(page 149)*

Part of the crop of female singer-songwriters that emerged in the mid-'90s to rule radio and the Lilith Fair circuit, Sarah McLachlan has been able to sustain her career by putting out consistent-selling records and chart-topping songs. "I Will Remember You" was the theme from the motion picture *The Brothers McMullen*, though the song may outlast the movie in the long run.

This song is in the key of A major and is one of the easier songs in this book. Starting off with a simple 1–4–5 progression, McLachlan begins her wistful ode to remembered love. She uses some slash chords in the verses as well as a couple of bars with different time signatures. Bar 6 is in 2/4, and when you listen to the song, feel the timing so you can make sure you have it right. Also notice how she starts the verse with a 1–4–1 chord pattern (A–D–A) but changes up the bass note to give the progression more movement. One of the great things about piano is that you can move the bass around with your left hand to create larger chords and motion within a piece of music.

This song has a lot of repetition, especially of the 1–4–5 chords. Make sure you're aware of the timing changes as you read the music. On the third page, you switch into an entire section in 2/4 before repeating back to the verse. Listen to the original recording of the song to reinforce how that timing sounds; that way when you play it, you know what you're trying to recreate. As the song comes to its conclusion, McLachlan repeats the intro part and winds it all up on the repeated line "Weep not for the memories." The bass line rises from D–E–F♯–G♯–A before setting up the 4–5–1 (D–E–A) resolution to the root chord. This is a pretty song that is meant to be played moderately slow, so take your time learning it.

I Write the Songs *(page 162)*

Perhaps the strangest fact about this song is that — gasp! — Barry Manilow didn't write it. Bruce Johnston from the Beach Boys has credit on this one. Though Manilow is responsible for countless originals ranging all the way back to the Coca-Cola jingle ("I'd Like to Teach the World to Sing") and the ever-popular "I Am Stuck on Band-Aids" song, a few of his greatest hits were covers. With its melancholy introduction, "I Write the Songs" is perhaps the greatest ode to songwriting on record. Writing a song about songwriting may seem redundant, but Manilow's honest vocal delivery and a huge orchestral arrangement made this a hit. Yet it still has great appeal even when played solo on the piano.

The upbeat bridge lifts the song up with some big major chords and even mentions some "rock and roll," probably the least common musical style found in Manilow's repertoire. The bridge does serve to deliver a heartfelt and bombastic final round of choruses wrapped in vocal ahhhs, strings, harps, horns and cymbal swells. When Manilow sings his last line, "I am music and I write the songs," the chords and music have lifted you to the pinnacle of emotion and given him a lofty platform on which to belt his final note. If you're unmoved by this sentimental crescendo, perhaps you need a long hug!

The song is in the key of F major, though the last chorus jumps two whole steps to A major, quite a leap for a key change. Johnston uses a special technique you might consider a sort of double resolution. You use a suspended chord to resolve to a dominant 7 chord, such as D7sus to D7, and then use that dominant 7 chord to resolve to a m2 chord, in this case Gm7. However, the biggest setup is the 5 chord (C major) at the end of the verse, which resolves back to the 1 (F) for the chorus. The 5–1 resolution is the most common in songwriting, simply because it works so well.

The chorus contains a huge hook and the chords underneath support it well. The chords and changes are fancied up with 7ths and slash chords, but realizing what the basic foundation is helps you understand the song much better. After all, a body without a skeleton has nothing to stand on! So if you cut to the bare structure of the chorus, you have a 1–m2–5–1 setup (F–Gm–C–F) under the first two lines, leading from 1 back to 1. Then you play a m6–2 change (Dm–G) and use the suspended chord to establish the G7. Interestingly, Johnston changes that major chord to the m2 (Gm7) and plays it over the C bass (5) using a mighty transition chord back to the 1 (F). That m2/5 transition chord (Gm7/C) is an encapsulation of the very common m2–5–1 setup that works so well to resolve to the root of a major key. You see that chord again in a repetitive pattern leading into the key change at the end of the bridge. In the final chorus, notice the chord changes: even though you are in a new key, you use the same numeric patterns. The Bm7/E chord at the end sets up the humongous resolution to the final A.

Imagine *(page 166)*

Of all the songs John Lennon wrote in his post-Beatles career, the song "Imagine" best encapsulates his wish for a world in which people are united in peace rather than divided by ideology, differences, and borders. This bold statement is still controversial to some who sought to have it banned after 9/11. Perhaps they enjoy a divided, warring world, but Lennon's vision lives on all these years later and remains a heartfelt plea for global unity.

The song is in the basic key of C major and is easy to play and sing. Perhaps John Lennon wanted people worldwide to enjoy it and spread the message. "Imagine" has a recognizable intro, starting with a simple progression of C–Cmaj7–F repeated twice. A little piano lick moves you back to the C that repeats through the song. The verse is basically the same chord progression as the introduction repeated under four lines of the lyric. After that, a short four-bar chorus begins on the F that ended the verse. The bass line descends from F–E–D–C before moving to a G chord. From the G you resolve back to the root chord (C major) that begins the verse again. The chords of the chorus are straight out of the C major scale and fall along the pattern 4–m6–m2–4–5 which is F–Am–Dm–F–G. Played with the bass line represented with the slash chords, you have a classic major key musical progression that is elegant in its simplicity. Also notice the last two bars of the chorus, in which Lennon uses a G–C/G–G7 progression. The C/G acts as a small resolution between the G and the G7, which sets up the larger resolution back to the root, C major.

From there, you move into another verse and chorus that move along the same progressions as before. The difference is that this time, when you end on the G7 of the chorus, you're leading into the bridge, where Lennon states "You may say that I'm a dreamer, but I'm not the only one." The progression here runs 4–5–1 (F–G–C) and then gives a great transition chord (E7) to lead from 1–4 (C–F).

Though the key of C major would use an E minor chord, this dominant 7th chord is one of the most popular non-scale transition chords between the 1 and the 4 chords. When you hear it and play it, you feel both the setup from C and the release to F. This happens three times before the simple ending of 4–5–1 (F–G–C) brings you home with a classic resolution. After this, you repeat a verse, chorus, and bridge after which Lennon finishes on the final root chord of C major.

It's Too Late (page 170)

Carole King was one of the most successful female singer-songwriters of the '70s, producing the classic *Tapestry* album in 1971 and opening the door to a wave of female artists. *Tapestry* had half a dozen hits and sold over 11 million records, cementing King's status as an artist. "It's Too Late" won a GRAMMY Award for Record Of The Year, and the album remained at #1 for 15 weeks. Though King had honed her chops writing songs with then-husband Gerry Goffin in the famous Brill Building through the late '60s, she was able to successfully transition to her own career as a songwriter and performer.

"It's Too Late" is a song made for playing on piano. It's in the easy key of C and is chock-full of pretty major 7th chords. The relative minor key of C major is A minor and this song relates more to the latter key. King opens with a simple Am7–D6 progression and plays a funky riff with it. Feel out the chords first and then apply the rhythm to them. Playing along with the song can help you dial in the feel of the part. The first four bars of the verse are over the same progression before leading to a descending chord pattern of Am7–Gm7–Fmaj7. The Gm is a departure from the key of C major, but it works with her melody here. The chorus starts with a back-and-forth progression of B♭maj7 to Fmaj7 and feels like it's in the key of F due to that feeling of resolution between the two chords. After the third repetition, King moves from the Fmaj7 to Dm7, setting up the Esus–Em7 chords as a mini-resolution leading to the larger resolution back to Am.

You then repeat the intro chords, verse, and chorus verbatim, before coming to the largely instrumental bridge. Off the Dm7 chord in the chorus, King leads you to an F/G–G7 setup to resolve to C major for the first time, a variation on the common 4–5–1 resolution. This feeling of landing on the major root chord is revelatory and gives a resolution that you haven't felt yet in the song.

The opening chords of the bridge are based on C–F–B♭, which is a descending series of 5ths (C is the 5 of F, F is the 5 of B♭) before descending down a chord pattern rooted in B♭–A–G–F. That F chord sets up the drop to Dm which leads to the E7sus–E7 set up for a return to Am. After this, King moves back to the original Am7–D6 progression, repeating it several times before setting up the chorus with the descending Am–Gm–F progression. That chorus leads back to the second ending, which starts the bridge chords. But instead of leading through a whole bridge, King moves from the Am7 chord before the coda to a more major key ending based on C major. She ends the song on a lovely Cmaj9 chord, bringing one of her biggest hits to a close. For those of you ending relationships, this song will always make you feel better!

Jump (page 174)

The opening chords of "Jump" signaled a turning point in Van Halen's illustrious career, as the world's current guitar hero showed up playing a synthesizer. An Oberheim OB-Xa synth, to be exact — a large '80s behemoth perfectly suited to the polyphonic fake-brass sound that would come to dominate mid-'80s keyboard sounds. That intro stands out decades later in such a way that from the first chord, there is no mistaking what song you're about to hear. Though Van Halen was a wild rock band fueled by the excesses of superstardom, this ditty became their first #1 hit and went on to be performed by bar mitzvah and wedding bands worldwide.

Though most people know Eddie Van Halen to be a guitar wunderkind, most don't realize that he was a classically trained pianist growing up, and didn't start playing guitar until his teens. So for those who cried "Heresy!" when Eddie hit the keys, they can now release their veneer of shock and realize that he's a well-rounded musician. In fact, knowing his history, it's amazing he didn't play keyboards sooner! Though singer David Lee Roth thought it would look like they were selling out to radio, Eddie knew he had a hit on his hands and stuck by his guns. Seeing as it was Van Halen's only #1 hit with Roth (they would have other hits later with replacement singer Sammy Hagar), it would seem that Eddie was proved right on this one.

Because "Jump" is in the key of C major, it's built mostly on the white keys, making it fairly easy to play. Follow the specific chord inversions in the sheet music to get the progression right. The verse follows the intro chords and plays mostly off the C major foundation. For the chorus, the song moves to the m6 chord (Am) before repeating a small descent from the 4 chord (F) down to the m2 chord (Dm) until eventually landing on the 5 chord (G) to set up the resolution back to 1 for the chorus. This is a classic 2–5–1 resolution, one of the most common in pop music.

The main song and the solo section are like two separate entities and should be approached as such. The solo section will take some work feeling through the fairly complex chord changes, which jump out of the key of C major. Even though the key signature doesn't change, think of these eight bars as if they were in D♭. The B♭m–G♭–A♭–D♭ progression then makes perfect sense — m6–4–5–1.

The second part of the solo moves back to the root key of C major to support the keyboard solo. For that solo, you play arpeggios over whole note bass notes. These arpeggios follow the chords listed above the staff notation. Thinking about those chords while you figure out the solo can help you understand how Van Halen structured it. You see a lot of F and G combinations (F/G and G/F); F and G are the 4 and 5 chords respectively in C major, so their use makes sense. However, the last part of the solo arpeggiates a Gsus chord over a descending chromatic bassline (B♭–A–A♭) before landing the solo on a C/G to resolve back to C major itself. After that, it's a straight repeat of the verse progression and a fade out. Try not to get frustrated learning the solo; Eddie Van Halen is an amazing musician and he sets the bar high! Good luck.

Listen to Your Heart (page 182)

The Swedish duo Roxette came out of nowhere (and have since returned) to unleash a gaggle of well-received hits on an unsuspecting public. In fact, they've released over 30 charting singles and sold over 45 million records worldwide! The duo of Per Gessle and Mats Persson wrote "Listen to Your Heart" back in 1988 for the album *Look Sharp*, and the song hit #1 in the United States, helping to sell 9 million albums in the process. Though their biggest U.S. successes may be behind them, they've certainly contributed to light rock radio stations nationwide.

The song is in the key of C major, though it bases itself on the relative key of A minor. The intro begins on the Am chord, then runs through Fsus2 and G5 to land on A5. (An A5 is an A chord without the 3rd. This is also known as a *power chord*. Because there is no 3rd, a power chord is able to adapt to a major or minor scenario.) After repeating a series of chords based on F–G–Am, you spring off of the Fsus2 to a Dm chord, which resolves back to the Asus2 that begins the verse. In the verse, you use the A–F–G–A framework of the intro beneath the somewhat esoteric lyrics — "the wake of your smile"?!? — winding up on Dm, which transitions into the chorus. The chorus uses more straightforward chords, beginning with two repetitions of the pattern Am–F–C–G. In the key of C major, that progression would be m6–4–1–5, which is a very common chord progression in pop and rock music. The rest of the chorus is a combination of those chords, ending on the Am that the song is really rooted in. After the chorus, you repeat the intro, verse, and chorus again with only subtle changes in the chords.

After the chorus repeat, you go to the coda, which uses a combination of the 1–4–5–m6 chords much like everything you've played before. The short instrumental section winds up on a G major chord and you arrive at a key change to D major. The bridge begins on a D major chord, beginning a pattern of 1–m6–5–4–5 (D–Bm–A–G–A) that makes sense in the context of the key, and is similar to the numerical progression you've seen in the song in its previous key.

But then, Roxette uses a B major chord as a transition to the next key change, a whole step up to E major, at which point you launch into the chorus. The progression (C♯m–A–E–B) is the same as before (m6–4–1–5). This is important to understand, so you can make sense of the basic foundation of the song. You finish with a repeating m6–4–5 progression, though the song ends on the m2 chord (F♯m), which leaves a bit of unresolved tension. Though this song goes through two key changes, the patterns remain very much the same throughout. Keeping that in mind can help you understand and ultimately perform the song comfortably.

Mandolin Rain (page 189)

Pianist/songwriter Bruce Hornsby had huge success with his multi-platinum debut album *The Way It Is,* on which the Top 5 hit song "Mandolin Rain" appeared, along with the smash title track. Hornsby did a stint as keyboardist with the Grateful Dead — though unlike their other keyboard players he actually survived, going on to enjoy a successful career with his band, The Range.

 This is a fairly straightforward song in the key of G major. Most of the chords fall within the G major scale and most of the progressions are common ones. Occasionally, Hornsby dresses up the basic chords with a suspended 2, a minor 7, or a slash chord with a different bass note, but the basic underlying structure remains the same. You can understand the Cmaj9/E in the verse by thinking of the more basic C/E, which is a helpful transition chord moving from D to G via the climbing D–E–G bass line. Paying attention to the fundamental structure helps you understand the song on a deeper level.

The only atypical chord Hornsby uses is the F major chord that begins the bridge. He only uses it twice, but it gives a nice changeup to differentiate the bridge from the rest of the song. At the end of the song, the direction says "Repeat and Fade," which could represent the last half of the song considering its length and repetitive nature. But Hornsby does a credible job of conjuring the wistful mood of the song and knows when to just let it roll on out. This song should be fairly easy to work out and can be extended as long as you desire.

Minute by Minute (page 196)

Back in the '70s — the "good old days" for many of us — The Doobie Brothers reigned supreme on rock radio, laying out such classic hits as "China Grove," "Listen to the Music," and the ever popular "Black Water." The addition of vocalist Michael McDonald gave the Doobies a unique sound that is served up on the hit song "Minute by Minute." This song is from the album of the same name, which also included the smash "What a Fool Believes."

This song is in the key of C major, though it does have a key change midway through. It's also in 12/8 time, which lends a kind of shuffle feel to the song. The intro rides quarter note chords over a walking octave bass. Practicing each hand separately makes the song easier to play when you put both hands together. The intro is a very gospel-influenced part, with a bass line that keeps climbing. Even though it's moving upward, when you go to the Am, you drop down and begin climbing again. That being said, the notes themselves are always moving upwards: D–E–F–F♯–G–G♯–A–B–C–C♯–D and so on, ending on the Dm7 in bar 6 to begin the slower funkier shuffle of the verse.

 Here you find a progression of Dm7–Dm7/G–Cmaj7 based on 2–2/5–1, a very common resolution. A quick F/G chord works to re-resolve the change into the root C major chord that begins the verse itself. These extra changes help establish the main chord changes through a chain of resolutions. Instead of a single straight 5–1 resolution, which would be G–C, you have Dm/G (2/5) resolving to the root chord (C major) and then a second, quick re-resolution from Cmaj7 to Cmaj7 using the F/G as a catalyst. Though these changes may not seem significant at first, their purpose is truly important.

The verse moves from C to variations on the F major chord, most notably F13sus. Don't get scared by the number 13; play the written chord and see how it sounds. The F chords are followed by Am/G–Dm7/G, using the m6–m2 change over a constant 5 bass (G). At the end of the verse, you transition chromatically through a G♭7 to the Fmaj7 that begins the chorus. The chorus works off chord variations on the pattern F–Dm/G–C (4–2/5–1), then follows the Cmaj7 with a chromatic descent (Bm–B♭–Am) to the next line beginning in Fmaj7. After a repeat of the F–Dm/G–C chord progression, you transition back to the beginning of the second verse with a quick 1–5–1 resolution using a F/G chord. After repeating a second verse and chorus, you find yourself at the chromatic descent (Bm–B♭–Am) into the instrumental intro section that is repeated here. The Am7 transitions nicely to the Dm7 chord that begins the intro section.

At the end of this instrumental section, the last chord (Dm7) works to transition to the Em7 that begins the bridge. Notice the key change to G major, which is closely related to the original key of C major. You use slash chords for every transition in the bridge. Without them, the chord structure would read Em7–Cmaj9–Am7–D7sus, which is based on the m6–4–m2–5 progression. Each of those transition chords works to set up the chord following it via motion in both the chord and the bass line, such as Am7–C/E–D7sus. The bridge ends on a descending chromatic chord progression (F♯m7–Fmaj7–E9) to get back to the chorus. The chorus still follows the 4–5–1 pattern but now in the G major scale that is represented by C–D–G. This chorus is followed by a descending progression (F♯–F–E) much like the one before the chorus. Though at this point it says "Repeat ad lib. and Fade," you are given an "optional ending" on the last page. This ending involves a repeat of the ascending, intro-section progression, which is now represented by a different set of chords along the G major scale.

The numerical chord formula of this ascending section hasn't changed, even though you are playing it in the new key. Again, practice each hand separately before trying it all together. The song ends on an Am7–C/D–G resolution that is a version of the 2–5–1 resolution you keep seeing in various songs. So start practicing your Michael McDonald impressions and enjoy the Doobies!

Rainy Days and Mondays (page 203)

The fourth of many million-selling singles for the brother-sister duo the Carpenters, "Rainy Days and Mondays" began its journey as a demo submitted by the songwriting team of Paul Williams and Roger Nichols, who were responsible for the huge hit "We've Only Just Begun" and many other chart-toppers. After the Carpenters recorded the definitive version of the song, they turned it into a huge hit. As you practice the song, Nichols's fantastic songwriting and chord construction become clear. He is truly an unsung hero on the list of great American songwriters.

This song has a lot of chord variation, so take some time to work through it and get comfortable playing it to speed. The song is in the key of E♭ major and the intro starts on the minor 6 chord (Cm). Feel through these changes slowly. Notice how Nichols uses a slash chord to transition the Fm7 to the E♭, and then he follows it up with a succession of slash chords over a constant bass note (B♭). He sets up the transition to the verse with a 1/5 chord (E♭/B♭) and then resolves it by way of the minor 2 chord (Fm7) to land gently on the 1 (E♭). The verse descends along the bass notes (E♭–D–D♭–C), and Nichols uses a very pretty Gm7♭5 chord.

Rather than dissect this song chord by chord, I focus on helping you grasp the fundamental structure here. Nichols likes to wind through changes; for instance, instead of a simple m2–5–1 change (Fm–B♭–E♭), he lays out m6–4–m2–5–1–m3–4–m2–5 in the bridge (Cm–A♭–Fm–B♭–E♭–Gm–A♭–Fm–B♭), giving a lot of movement around the 1. He also resists a straight resolution on the hook where, instead of resolving to an E♭ chord, he finishes in a string of chords played over the 5 (B♭) bass note. That lets the next verse, which starts on the 1 chord (E♭), take the role of the ultimate resolution. Tricks like these make these songs both fresh and long-lasting in the pop songbook.

In the coda, the song changes keys to F major, a whole step up. Notice how the chord progression sounds and feels the same. The numerical formula underneath doesn't change even though the root key does. After you start thinking about progressions numerically, not only will they make more sense, but you'll be able to transpose them into any key you want. And that can only be a good thing! In the meantime, don't let those rainy days and Mondays get you down.

Still the Same (page 208)

Bob Seger came out of Detroit on a mission to populate rock radio with scores of hits, and he succeeded wildly. From staples like "Night Moves" and "Against the Wind" to the rocking "Katmandu" and "Old Time Rock & Roll," Seger's brand of American rock 'n' roll found a receptive audience nationwide. From the 1978 album *Stranger in Town,* the song "Still the Same" is his ode to all the overachievers in Hollywood, though the song can be interpreted in a variety of ways. The song was recorded as a trio with just piano, bass, and drums, making it a very simple arrangement to learn and play.

The song is in the key of C major and sticks to very basic chords. The opening progression is very simple and recognizable, leading along the 1–m3–5 pattern of C–Em–G. This pattern continues under the first two lines of the verse, after which Seger moves from 4–5–1 (F–G–C). He then uses an E major chord which sets up the resolution to the following Am chord. That in turn sets up the progression Am–Dm–G, which neatly resolves back to the C major chord that begins the second verse. Notice that there is no chorus between verses 1 and 2. After the second verse, which is the same as the first, you hit the chorus on the major C root chord. Seger then uses the E major chord but instead of Am like before, he transitions to an A major chord, which has a distinctly upbeat feel. That A major chord is meant to set up the Dm–G–C resolution.

 I use the word *resolution* a lot, but that is the key to how chord progressions work in creating and releasing tension. The common setup and resolution of m2–5–1, like you see in the Dm–G–C progression, works very well and is used in countless pop songs.

After a third half-instrumental verse, you play a chorus and follow it up with an outro section that rotates the C–Em–G progression that you played in the song's intro. Repeat this section and instead of fading out, end on the C major chord, giving the song the ultimate final resolution. This is truly a fun and easy song to play on the piano, so enjoy it!

The Stranger (page 212)

Billy Joel's mid-'70s output was among his strongest, both artistically and commercially, and 1977's *The Stranger* is regarded as one of his best. The title song, perhaps an emotional counterpoint to the Top 10 hit "Just the Way You Are," was an ode to estranged relationships, of which Joel has had his share. The song starts and ends with a jazzy piece that nicely counters the more rock-oriented song itself. Legend has it that Joel whistled his idea to producer Phil Ramone, who decided that, instead of another instrument, Joel should stick with whistling the part. Thus, a classic was born.

The song is in the key of G major, though it relates more to the relative key of E minor. Joel doesn't stick to the fundamental scale chords, using an E major chord in the fifth bar and a transitory E7♭9/G♯ chord to segue to the Am in the next bar. Then he leads a descending progression of slash chords that transition well into one another. The change from B minor to B major in bar eight helps resolve back to the Em chord. The second half of the intro uses a similar progression to the first half but if you compare the two, you may notice how Joel uses some different chord variations. He also changes the descending progression, winding it down to the 5/4 chord (B/A) that resolves back to the Em.

The outro of the song is actually the second half of the intro, note for note — so when you get there, you already know what you're doing!

The rock part of the song kicks off with a funky back and forth between Em and C7. The verse chords are fairly straightforward, staying along the chords of the Em scale: Em–F#dim–G–Am–Bm–C–D. Notice that there is no true chorus in this song, just a mention of the Stranger at the end of every verse. When you get to the bridge, Joel reaches for a Gmaj7 then drops the third to the minor before leading down to the D/F# that begins the rest of the line. That line turns around on an Am7–D–G, which is the common m2–5–1 chord resolution. When he repeats the progression in the second half, he leads down to D but keeps descending to D7/C and then veering further down to the Bm7. That chord transitions down chromatically through the B♭+ to the A6 before jumping to a B7♭9, which provides a great segue to the Em of the next verse. Joel can sometimes move quickly through his chord progressions, but if you take them slow, you'll become comfortable with them.

You finish out the rock part with a repeated verse and bridge, jamming out on the Em–C7 progression that makes up the verse. This fades into the outro section which gives you a chance to wistfully whistle Joel's melancholy melody and bring the song to a close on a B–B/A–Em resolution. Learn this song section by section before putting it all together and you'll be jamming it in no time!

Superman (It's Not Easy) (page 220)

Though some say Five for Fighting's Jon Ondrasik sounds a bit like a Muppet, quite a few people obviously like his music and have bought his records out the whazoo. This song was a big hit for the band and further established Ondrasik as a songwriter. The song's lyrics are written from the point of view of Superman, who seems to feel insecure in his abilities to be, well, super. (Maybe he needs to hear you play "I Believe I Can Fly" more often.) A stretch, sure, but perhaps Ondrasik was alluding to the strength we all have to find within ourselves to rise above our situations and be superheroes of our own.

This song is in the key of C major, the easiest key to play in on the piano. Throughout the song, Ondrasik takes the root chords and dresses them up a bit. Instead of a G, you get a G5. Instead of an F, you get an Fsus2 or an F(add9), which are really not that different when you play them. So when you look at the root foundations of the chords, you see the intro pattern as 1–5–m6–4 (C–G–Am–F) repeated twice. The verse continues that exact pattern three times, winding up the fourth line with a 1–5–4–1 progression that ends back on the root chord of C major. There is one bar of 2/4 near the end of the verse. If the counting is confusing, listen to the original recording and this will fall under your fingers easily. Also to be noted is the lack of a cohesive chorus section. Instead, what you get is the last line of the verse ("It's not easy being me") working as the chorus/tag line.

The second verse is roughly the same for the first eight bars, but then Ondrasik changes up a little bit with a descending bass line along the established chord progression. So instead of C–G–Am–F, you see a slash chord on the G with a B in the bass, creating a descending C–B–A–F bass pattern. A slight difference to be sure, but worth noting nonetheless. Other than that difference, the verse finishes out the same.

You then transition into a bridge section via that same descending pattern of C–G/B–Am, which then rises right back up that same pattern in reverse (Am–G/B–C). From that C major chord, you move to Dm and then Am, which makes a 1–m2–m6 progression that you use to transition to a D major chord. That D chord stands out a bit because it's the first non-scale chord so far in the song. You repeat it again two bars later before transitioning out of the bridge with a common 4–5–1 resolution to the root chord (F–G–C) for the next verse. This verse works by the same principles of the ones before it, so you aren't in foreign territory. The song ends on predictable chords, winding up on the root chord of C major. Though the song is easy to play, it will surely test out your falsetto singing range. Prepare to hit those high notes, Superman!

A Thousand Miles (page 228)

Vanessa Carlton came virtually out of nowhere with "A Thousand Miles," which got GRAMMY nominations for Record Of The Year and Song Of The Year, but lost out on both to Norah Jones. (See "Don't Know Why.") Still, a nomination is nothing to sneeze at!

This song is meant to be played on piano and it has a very involved part full of sixteenth-note arpeggios that must be learned slowly to get up to speed. Trying to learn this song at full speed is counterproductive. Rather, take the time to figure it out slowly, and, most importantly, find your fingering. The right fingering can make this song sound as natural for you as it does for Vanessa herself.

The song is in the key of B♭ major but it spends very little time on the root chord. Some of the magic of this song is how it doesn't always resolve to the root, which leaves a sort of tension that never quite dissipates. It's a good tool of songwriting and part of building tension-release situations by resolving, or, in this case, not resolving, to root chords. The verse is an excellent example. Carlton plays around with many E♭ and F chords, but doesn't resolve to B♭. Keep in mind that E♭ and F are the 4 and 5 chords in B♭. 4–1 and 5–1 resolutions are very strong. Not using these strong resolutions creates a sense of continuous motion and tension. In fact, the only time you see the root chord (B♭) during the song is as a B♭/D slash chord, which doesn't really establish itself due to its combination with the bass note (D).

The instrumental intro starts out on E♭ and circles back to itself through a series of short transitional chord changes. The E♭–F–B♭/D–E♭ progression loops three times and then Carlton sets up the first verse with the Fsus–Dm–E♭6 progression. The verse chords are very similar to the intro, though the piano part itself is different. The first line of the verse is followed by an instrumental line, and then repeated. That second line of the verse ends with a transition into the chorus. The E♭5 you had been playing becomes an E♭sus2, followed by a B♭ chord with a descending bass line (F–D). So, you have this motion of E♭ with the bass circling around it with a staccato chord pattern over the E♭–F–D bass rotation. The fourth bar has an E♭(add9) — which is really similar to the E♭sus2 it replaces — moving to a straight F chord.

Throughout this song, you play several versions of the E♭ chord that deserve explanation. E♭6 is composed of the 1, 3, 5, and 6 notes of the scale. E♭5 uses the 1 and 5 notes. E♭sus2 is made up of the 1, 2, and 5 notes. Sometimes the chord names can be confusing, so review them in the staff notation to better understand what you're playing.

The chorus is four lines, the first three of which are the same. The first bar is a combination of F and E♭ chords, whereas the second bar works from Dm–B♭/D back to more F and E♭ variations. Under this chord pattern, notice the bass, which follows E♭–F–D–E♭ similar to the chorus. After three times through, the E♭sus2 transitions to Gm7, then Dm7/A and finally F. In the key of B♭ major (which you're still in) that would be a progression of 4–m6–m3/7–5, which leaves you unresolved, and nowhere near the root. The F steps down into the opening riff, which works around that rotating bass line (E♭–F–D–E♭). This in turn enters into another verse and chorus. After that second chorus, there is a short repeat of the instrumental intro before you enter a kind of bridge section. Carlton follows a climbing pattern from Gm7–F/A–F/B♭–Cm6, using the lift in the bass (G–A–B♭–C) under the m6–5–m2 chords (Gm–F–Cm) and ending the last time on the F/A–F7sus combination that returns you to the original verse. After this last verse you jump to the coda, which has a twice-repeated chorus that stretches the last line out for maximum emotional impact over the Gm7–F/A–F chords, leaving you on the 5 chord once again.

Interestingly, at the very end, Carlton takes all the pent-up tension and releases it in 4 bars full of B♭ resolution. Under the same piano part as the intro, she plays three variations of B♭ changing to the 4 (E♭) in each of the first three lines before landing on B♭sus–B♭–B♭sus. That last "sus" takes the resolution and adds a little question mark to it, showing you that, with Vanessa, some things are never truly resolved.

Walking in Memphis (page 236)

Marc Cohn won the 1991 GRAMMY for Best New Artist based on this exuberant ode to Memphis, Tennessee. Cohn wrote the song after seeing Al Green preach in Memphis, and he filled it with the kind of imagery that make Tennessee and the Deep South so interesting. He references Beale Street, which is a famous street in Memphis' musical history, as well as W.C. Handy, a blues musician immortalized in the area with a big festival and a flattering statue. There are more inside references to dig into, but for now, you can dig into the song itself.

This song is in the key of C major, which is the easiest key to learn on piano. With the exception of a few chords in the bridge, every chord in this song comes from the C major scale. The song opens with a four-bar introduction that has a simple triplet part in the right hand. Cohn uses a lot of 5 chords (F5, G5, A5, etc.), which means he's leaving out the third and playing just the 1 and 5 notes.

The 1 and 5 notes don't change whether a chord is minor or major. For example, A major is A–C♯–E and A minor is A–C–E; both use the notes A and E. Because the third is how you determine whether a chord is minor or major, these third-less chords can work over a major or minor scale with no problem.

You begin the song by repeating the chord pattern F–G–C–A twice, then use that pattern under the entire verse using the third-less 5 chords the whole way. When you kick into the chorus, thirds are added to differentiate the section. You have a slight variation on the verse chords, playing off the Am to a straight F–G–C–Am progression. At the end of the chorus, the F–G lead into a short, two-bar instrumental section before moving into a second verse. This verse is a bit different from the first in that you don't play an A chord until the tenth bar, and when you do, it's a straight Am. The chord foundation itself is different, moving down from G–F–C/E–Dm and repeating that descent until the tenth bar when Cohn settles on a straight C major chord to begin the second half of the verse. This second half works off the progression 1–m6–4–5 (C–Am–F–G) before leading into the chorus, which uses very similar chords. At the end of this second chorus, you land on a C7sus–C7 progression that begins the bridge.

The bridge has a distinct gospel feel, and with good reason, considering the subject matter. After six repetitions of the C7sus–C7 chords, Cohn slows down to lead you through a progression that runs E7–F7–F♯dim–G7. He plays this section freely, meaning without a steady beat, so you're free to give it your own feel and timing. The added 7ths in the chords, the dim chord, the chromatic bass line (E–F–F♯–G), and the free tempo all serve to give this section a strong gospel feel. The last chord (G7) leads into a repeat of the instrumental intro section and another verse. Some of the chords differ from the first verse, such as the G7sus instead of a G5 chord, but it adds to the gospel flavor of the lyrics. Cohn leads into a final chorus that repeats before revisiting the instrumental intro section. After this, you repeat the first two lines of the first verse before playing the outro section. You end on an F–Gsus–G–C progression that sets up the resolution to the root chord of C major. After you've strolled through this song, you may feel like a visit to Graceland yourself.

You Are So Beautiful (page 246)

One of the most beautiful love songs of all time, "You Are So Beautiful" was actually co-written by infamous keyboardist (and fifth Beatle) Billy Preston. However, it was Joe Cocker's aching rendition that pushed the song to a Top 5 hit in 1975. Since then, this song has been sung at countless weddings and inspired many men to serenade their ladies with its charming and simple melody. And because Joe's voice cracks on the high notes, you don't have to try and sing this song perfectly. In fact, the more tortured your vocal performance, the better. You wouldn't want the love of your life thinking you weren't truly committed, would you?

The song is in the key of A♭ major, which is going to involve a lot of black keys. Relax — black keys are your friends! The chord progression is fairly repetitive, so after you get the gist of it you're on your way. Starting with the root chord of A♭ major, the song opens with a descending progression to the 4 chord (D♭). This progression repeats before you return to the root for the beginning of the verse. In bar 5, you see a descent from A♭ to A♭maj7 to A♭7, leading you through a nice setup to the pretty 4 chord (D♭maj7) under the word "beautiful." The G♭9 that comes next doesn't directly come from the A♭ major scale, but it works really well to transition back to the root chord. The progression is repeated, and then you enter the second section of the song.

You start down the same path of A♭ to A♭maj7 but then are given an E♭m to transition to an A♭7. This is all meant to build anticipation as you get to that D♭maj7 that follows. That chord then gives way to the C7 in the first bar of the third page and you get a one-bar sequence where you go from C7 to C+ and back to C7. This helps build the C7 for the next resolution to Fm. Remember that building and releasing the tension through the resolution of chord changes is what gives a song motion and enhances the emotional impact of the lyric. After you hit that Fm, you have a descending series of 7ths setting up the pretty B♭9, which in turn releases you back to the root of A♭ and starts the verse over again. After you get to the second ending and hit that Fm chord again, you transition to a freely played B♭13♯11 chord.

Now, that has to be the longest chord name you'll see in this whole book, but don't let it scare you! This is an expansive chord that is meant to be arpeggiated with two hands, creating a big build up before releasing you back to the root chord. Play it harmonically (all together) and then melodically (one note at a time) and try to understand what you're playing. After you resolve to the A♭, you have one more revolution of the main chord progression before ending on the root chord, giving a perfect resolution to a beautiful song.

You Are the Sunshine of My Life (page 250)

The opening track from *Talking Book*, Stevie Wonder's second album, went to #1 in 1972 and secured Wonder a GRAMMY for Best Male Pop Vocal. The other monster hit on the record, the double-GRAMMY-winning "Superstition," is as funky and energetic as "Sunshine of My Life" is beautiful and pretty, showing the depth and breadth of Wonder's musical style.

After his split from Motown Records, Wonder began writing some of his best-known hits, and "Sunshine" was certainly a big one. It is in the key of C major, which is the easiest key to play because it uses all the white keys. Yet Wonder uses a plethora of chords that use notes outside of the scale and shows how coloring outside of the lines can be remarkably striking and beautiful.

The intro starts on a Cmaj9 with a pattern of two notes in the right hand against an octave in the left. That two-note pattern climbs in the second two bars through a G7♯5 chord, passing through several notes that are not actually part of a G7♯5 chord. The G is the 5 of C and sets up the resolution to the 1 chord (C) in the chorus (bar five). Most of the chords are straight out of the C major scale, except the G♭/B♭, which works as a transition chord between the Em7 and the Dm7 in bar eight. When you get to the transition to the verse, you'll play a G13♭9 as part of a 2–5–1 resolution (Dm–G–C). Don't worry about the fancy name; just play the chord as notated on the staff and you'll hear how well it transitions to the C major chord following it.

The verse also uses chords from the C major scale, though you'll play with the E chords on the top of the third page to work a transition between F major and A major. Play through these changes and feel how they build up to the A. After that, notice how you move from the A major to an A minor through the D and E chords; that Am sets up the D7, which in turn sets up the G7, which then sets up the return to C major in the chorus, creating a m6–2–5–1 resolution. Recognize this for what it is — one big setup to resolve to the chorus. Though some of the chords can get jazzy, "Sunshine" is a fairly straightforward song that is easy to play.

Against All Odds (Take a Look at Me Now)

Words and Music by Phil Collins

Moderately slow

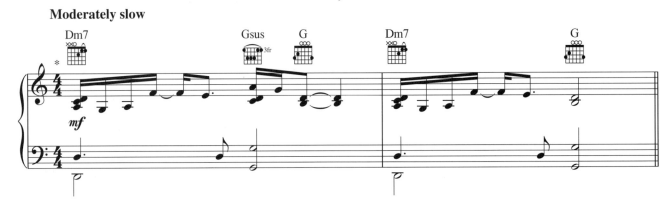

How can I just let you walk a - way, just let you leave with - out___ a trace, when I

stand here tak - ing ev - 'ry breath___ with you?___ Ooh.___ You're the

Recorded a half step lower.

on - ly one who real - ly knew me___ at all.___

How can you just walk a - way from me, when all I can do is watch you leave?_ 'Cause we've
wish I could just make you turn a - round, turn a - round and see me cry.___ There's so

shared the laugh - ter and___ the pain,_ and e - ven shared___ the tears.___ You're the
much I need___ to say___ to you,_ so man - y rea - sons why.___ You're the

well, there's just an emp-ty space, and you com-ing back _
'cause there's just an emp-ty space. _ But to wait _

_ to me _ is a - gainst _ the odds, _ and that's what _ I've got _ to face. _
_ for you _ is all _ I can do, _ and that's what _

I _ I've got _ to face. _ Take a good look at me now, _

Alone

Words and Music by Billy Steinberg and Tom Kelly

*Recorded a half step lower.

Back at One

Words and Music by Brian McKnight

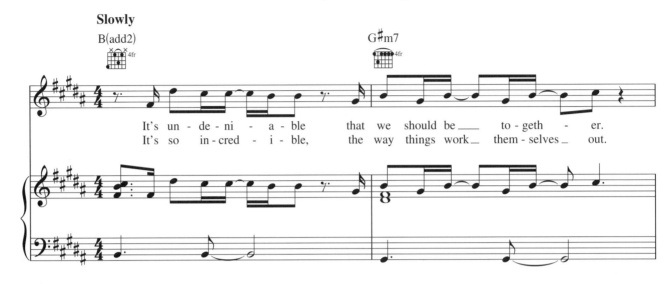

It's un-de-ni-a-ble that we should be ___ to-geth-er.
It's so in-cred-i-ble, the way things work ___ them-selves ___ out.

It's un-be-liev-a-ble how I used to say ___ that I'd fall nev-er.
And all e-mo-tion-al, once you know what ___ it's all a-bout, hey.

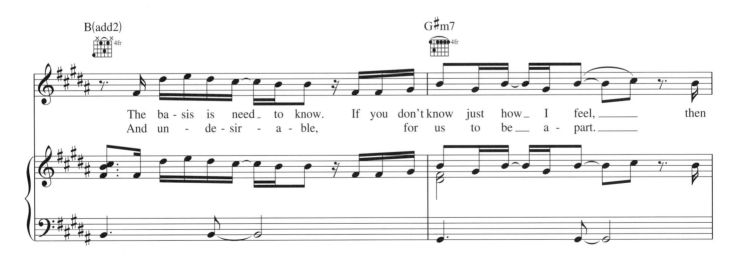

The ba-sis is need ___ to know. If you don't know just how ___ I feel, ___ then
And un-de-sir-a-ble, for us to be a-part. ___

Candle in the Wind

Music by Elton John
Words by Bernie Taupin

Changes

Words and Music by David Bowie

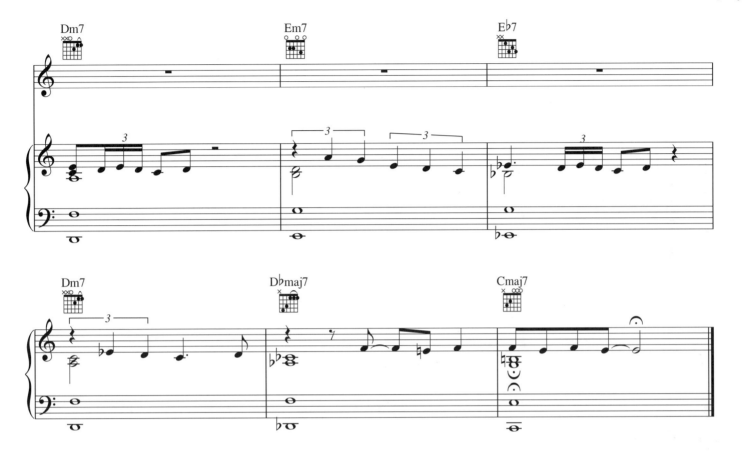

Additional Lyrics

2. I watch the ripples change their size, but never leave the stream
   Of warm impermanence and so the days flowed through my eyes
   But still the days seem the same.
   And these children that you spit on as they try to change their worlds
   Are immune to your consultations, they're quite aware of what they're going through.

   (Ch-ch-ch-ch-Changes) Turn and face the strange.
   (Ch-ch-changes) Don't tell them to grow up and out of it.
   (Ch-ch-ch-ch-Changes) Turn and face the strange.
   (Ch-ch-changes) Where's your shame? You've left us up to our necks in it.
   Time may change me, but you can't trace time.

Clocks

Words and Music by Guy Berryman, Jon Buckland, Will Champion and Chris Martin

Moderately

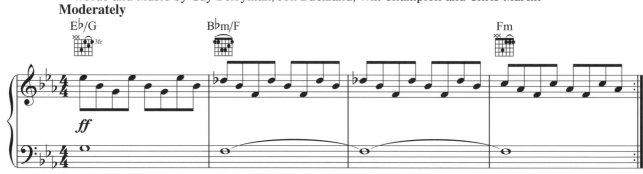

Lights go out and I can't be saved. __ Tides that I tried to
Con - fu - sion __ nev - er stops. __ Clos - ing __ walls and

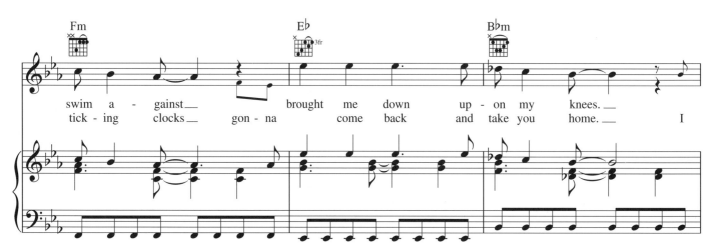

swim a - gainst __ brought me down up - on my knees. __
tick - ing clocks __ gon - na come back and take you home. __ I

And noth - ing else com - pares.

D.S. al Coda
(with repeats)

Come Sail Away

Words and Music by Dennis DeYoung

Don't Know Much

Words and Music by Barry Mann, Cynthia Weil and Tom Snow

Don't Know Why

Words and Music by Jesse Harris

Dreamer

Words and Music by Rick Davies and Roger Hodgson

lot I can do.

Bb/C

C

(Work it out some - day.)

Bb/C

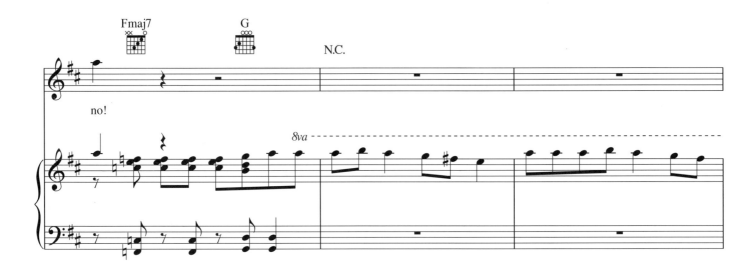

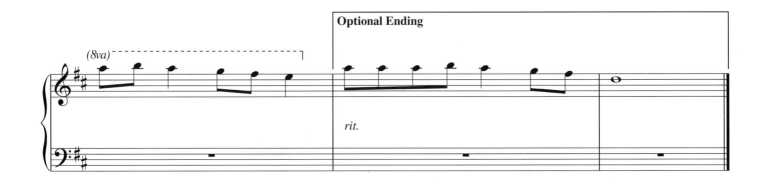

Drops of Jupiter (Tell Me)

Words and Music by Pat Monahan, Jimmy Stafford, Rob Hotchkiss, Charlie Colin and Scott Underwood

Fallin'

Words and Music by Alicia Keys

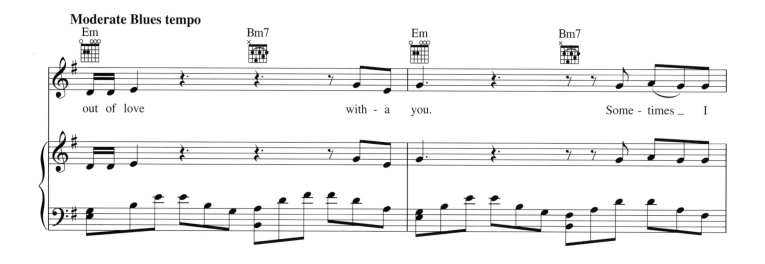

love with-a you. I _____ nev - er loved some - one ____ the way that

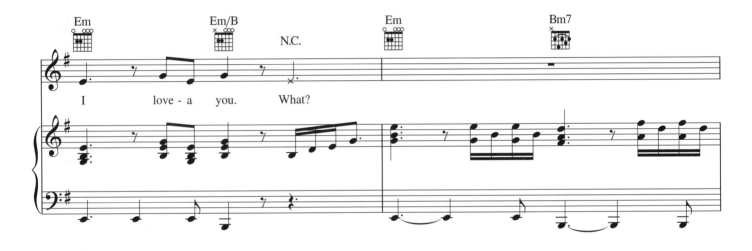

I love - a you. What?

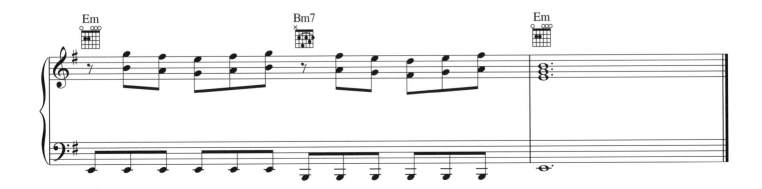

Good Vibrations

Words and Music by Brian Wilson and Mike Love

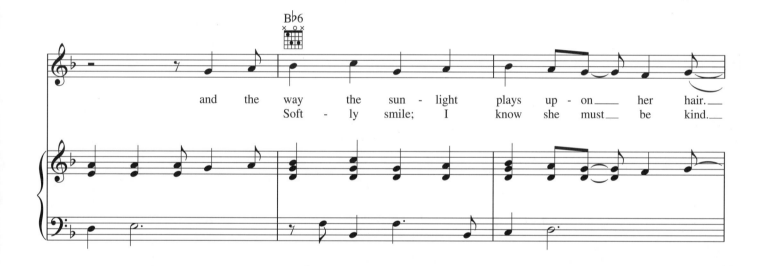

Original key: E♭ minor. This edition has been transposed down one half-step to be more playable.

Hard to Say I'm Sorry

Words and Music by Peter Cetera and David Foster

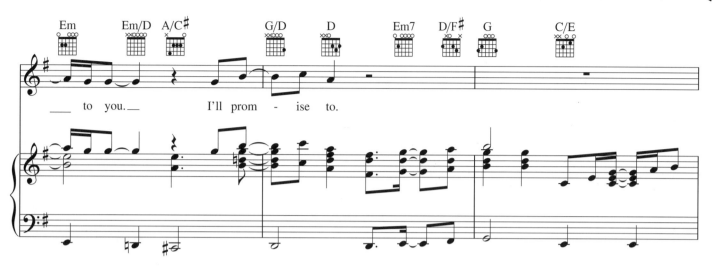

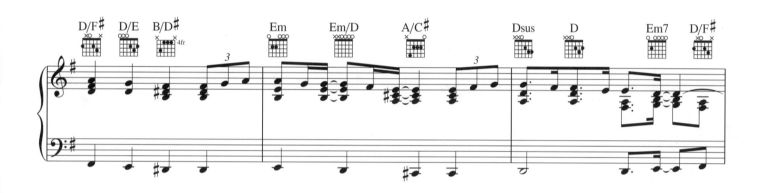

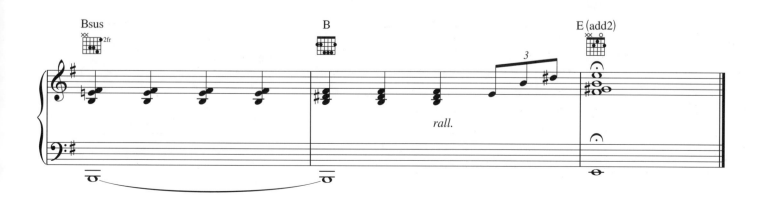

Have I Told You Lately

Words and Music by Van Morrison

Hello

Words and Music by Lionel Richie

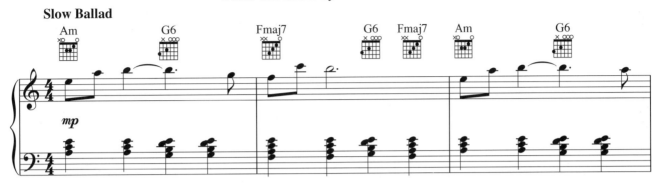

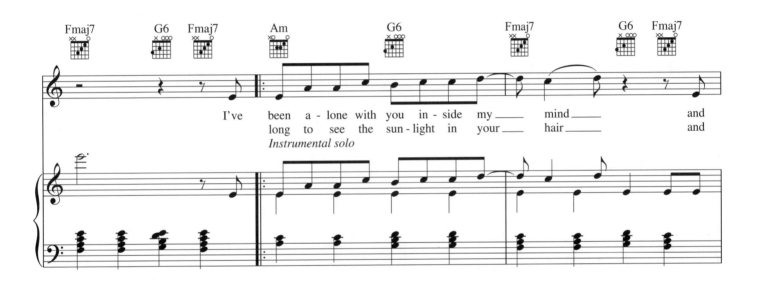

I've been a - lone with you in - side my _____ mind _____ and
long to see the sun - light in your _____ hair _____ and
Instrumental solo

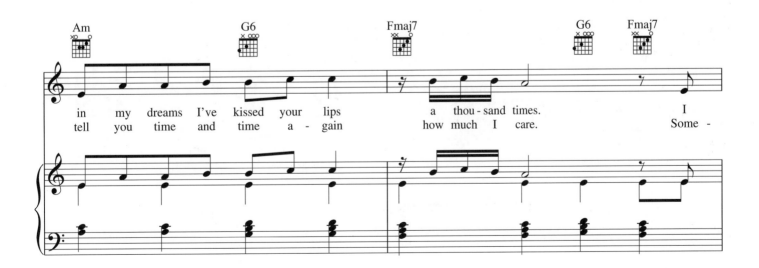

in my dreams I've kissed your lips a thou - sand times. I
tell you time and time a - gain how much I care. Some -

Hey Jude

Words and Music by John Lennon and Paul McCartney

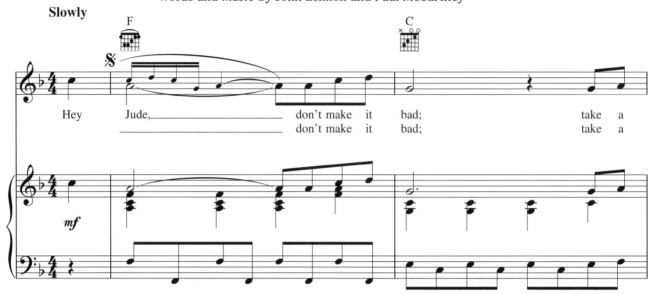

I Believe I Can Fly

Words and Music by Robert Kelly

(Everything I Do) I Do It for You

from the Motion Picture ROBIN HOOD: PRINCE OF THIEVES

Words and Music by Bryan Adams, Robert John Lange and Michael Kamen

I Will Remember You

Theme from THE BROTHERS McMULLEN
Words and Music by Sarah McLachlan, Seamus Egan and Dave Merenda

Moderately slow

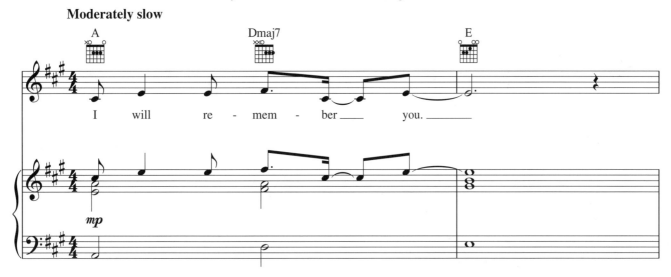

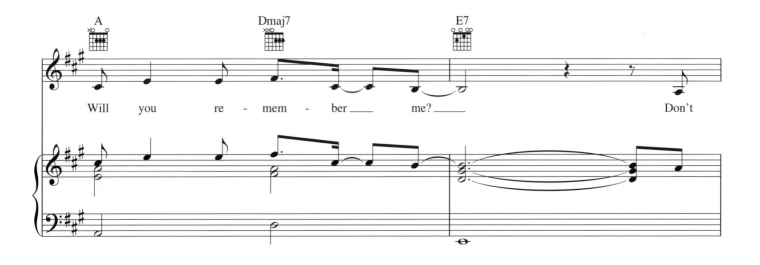

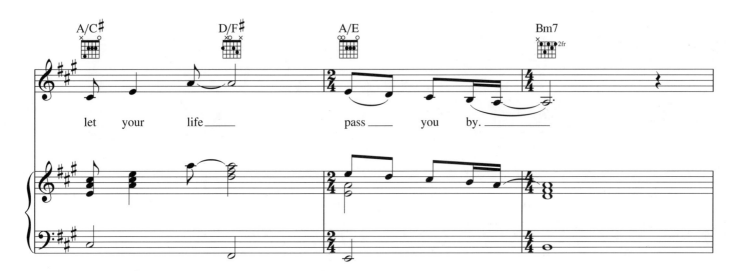

I Don't Want to Wait

Words and Music by Paula Cole

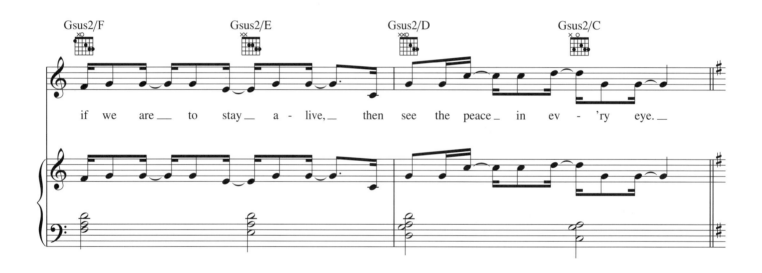

So o-pen up___ your morn - ing light___ and say a lit - tle prayer___ for I.___ You know that if we are___ to stay___ a - live,___ then see the love___ in ev - 'ry eye.___

Repeat and Fade

I Write the Songs

Words and Music by Bruce Johnson

Imagine

Words and Music by John Lennon

It's Too Late

Moderately slow

Words and Music by Carole King and Toni Stern

Stayed in bed all morn-in' just to pass the time. ___
used to be so eas-y, liv-in' here with you. ___

There's some-thin' wrong here, there can be no de-ny-in'. One of us ___ is chang-in', or
You were light and breez-y, an' I knew just what to do. Now you look so un-hap-py, and I ___

may-be we've just ___ stopped try - in'. ___
___ feel ___ like a fool. ___

And it's too ___

Jump

Words and Music by David Lee Roth, Edward Van Halen, Alex Van Halen and Michael Anthony

Bright Rock

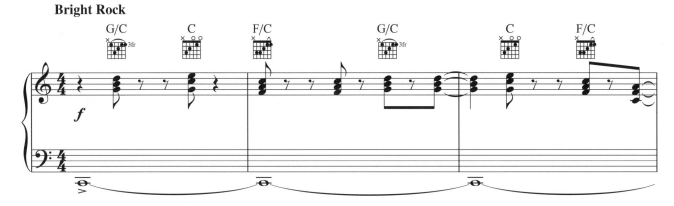

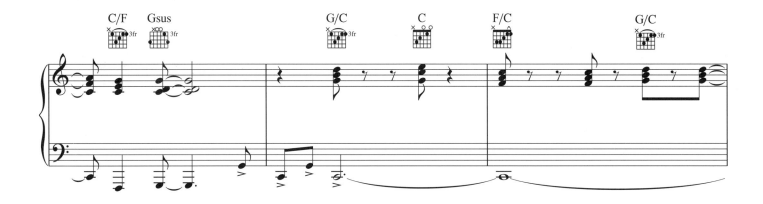

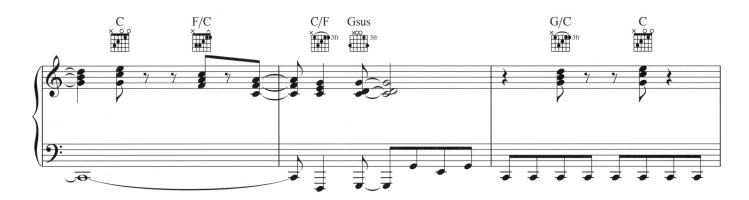

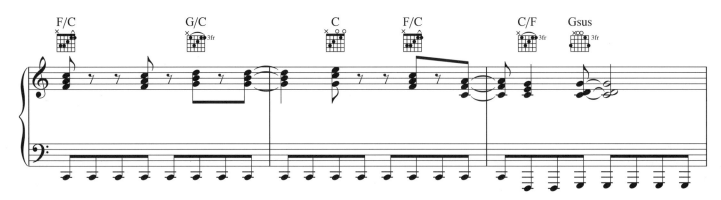

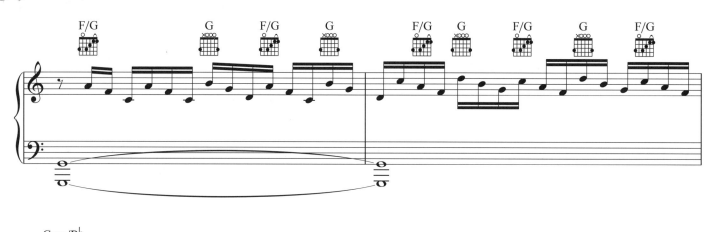

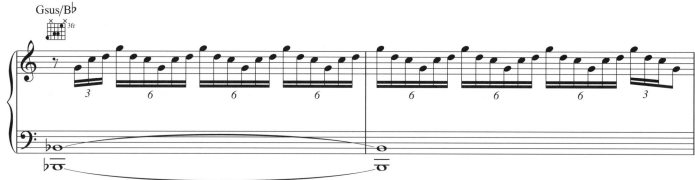

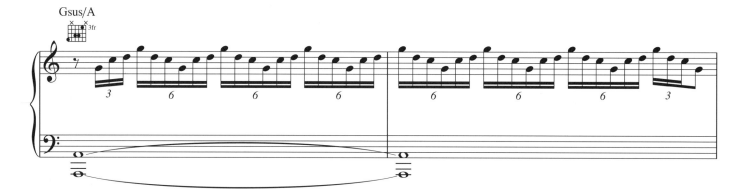

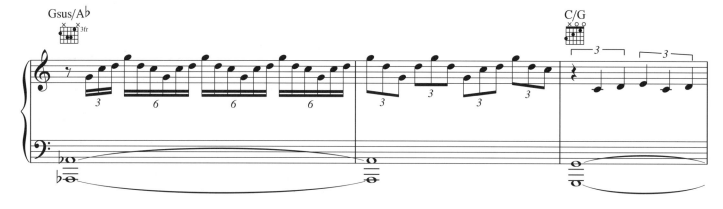

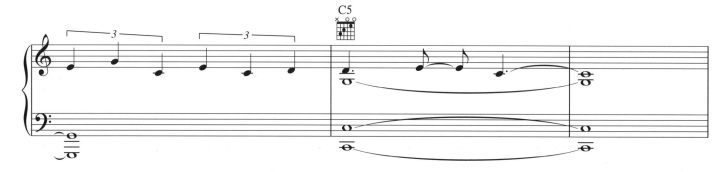

Listen to Your Heart

Words and Music by Per Gessle and Mats Persson

Mandolin Rain

Words and Music by B.R. Hornsby and John Hornsby

Moderately slow

The

song   came   and   went   like   the   times   that   we   spent ___   hid - ing   out
cool   eve - ning   dance,   lis - t'nin'   to   the   blue grass   band,   takes   the   chill ___
boat's   steam - ing   in.   Oh,   I   watch   the   side wheel   spin ___   and   I   think ___

_____   from   the   rain ___   un - der   the   car - ni - val   tent. ___
_____   from   the   air ___   un - til   they   play   the   last   song. _____
_____ a - bout ___ her   when _____   I   hear   that   whis - tle   blow. _____

I

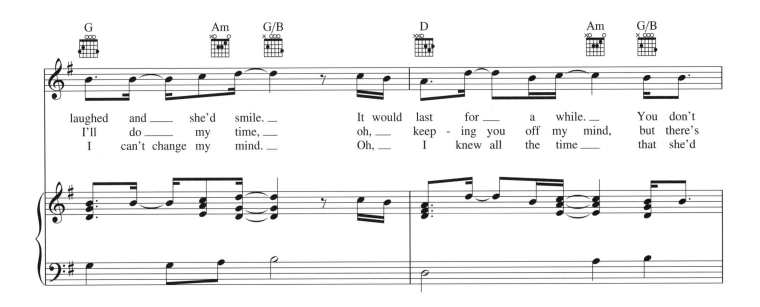

laughed   and ___   she'd   smile. ___   It   would   last   for ___   a   while. ___   You   don't
I'll   do ___   my   time, ___   oh,   keep - ing   you   off   my   mind,   but   there's
I   can't change   my   mind. ___   Oh, ___   I   knew   all   the   time ___   that   she'd

know ____ what you got ____ till you lose it all ____ a - gain. ____
mo - ments that I find ____ I'm not feel - ing so strong.
go ____ but that's a choice. I made long a - go.

Lis - ten to the

man - do - lin rain. ____ Lis - ten to the mu - sic on the lake. Oh, lis - ten to my

heart break ____ ev - 'ry time she runs ____ a - way. ____ Oh, lis - ten to the

ban - jo wind, ____ a sad song drift - ing low. Lis - ten to the

Lis - ten to the tears roll_____ down my face as she

turns to ___ go. Lis - ten to the tears_____ roll down my face as she

turns to go._____

Repeat and Fade

Optional Ending

Minute by Minute

Words by Michael McDonald and Lester Abrams
Music by Michael McDonald

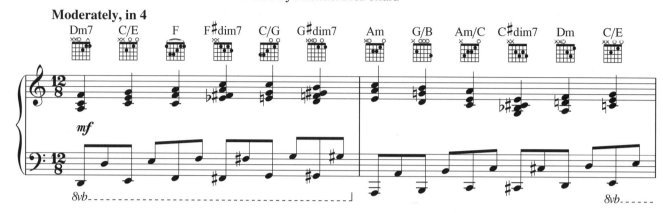

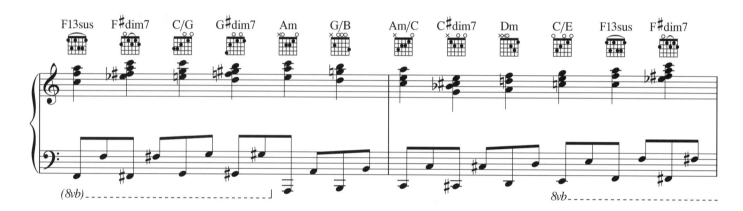

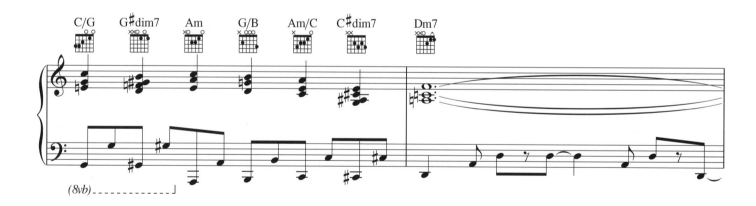

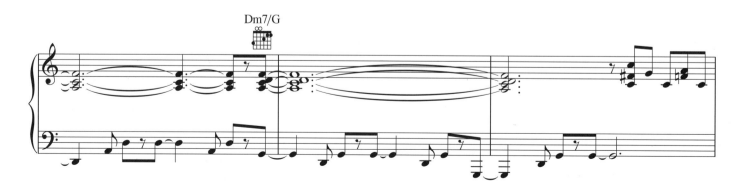

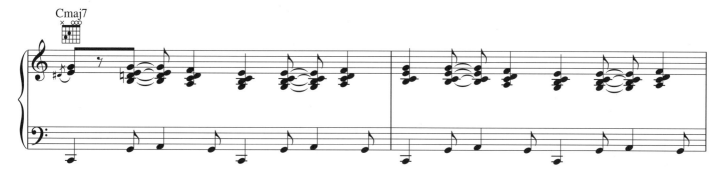

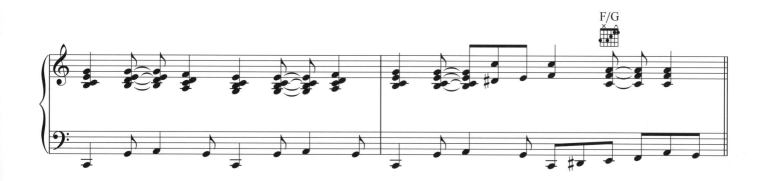

Hey,___ don't___ wor - ry; I've been lied___ to.
You___ would___ stay just to watch me, dar - ling,

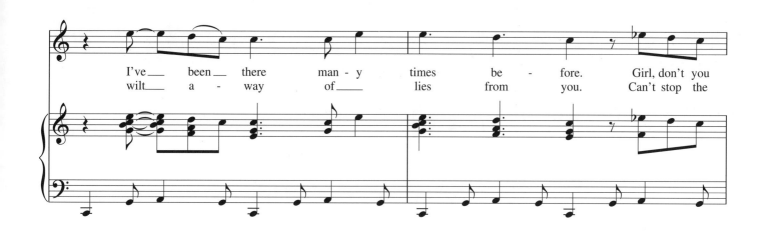

I've___ been there man - y times be - fore. Girl, don't you
wilt___ a - way of ___ lies from you. Can't stop the

Rainy Days and Mondays

Lyrics by Paul Williams   Music by Roger Nichols

Still the Same

Words and Music by Bob Seger

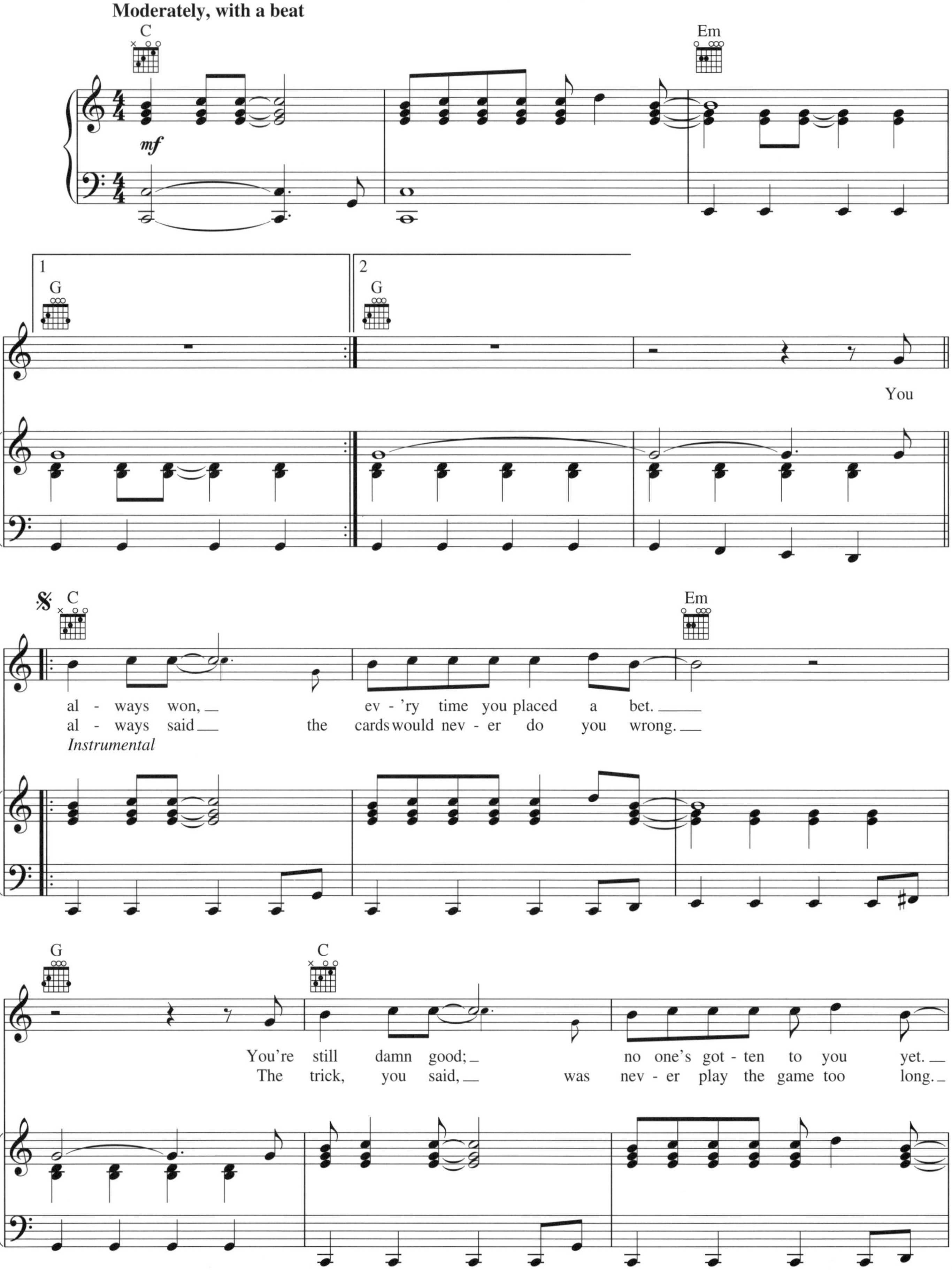
Moderately, with a beat
C
Em
mf
1
G
2
G
You
C
Em
al - ways won, ev - 'ry time you placed a bet.
al - ways said the cards would nev - er do you wrong.
Instrumental
G
C
You're still damn good; no one's got - ten to you yet.
The trick, you said, was nev - er play the game too long.

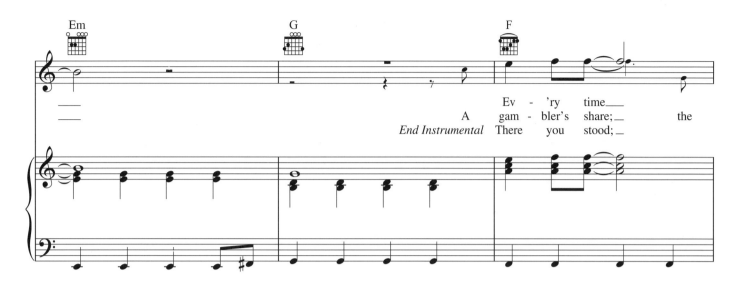

Ev - 'ry time___
A gam - bler's share;___ the
End Instrumental There you stood;___

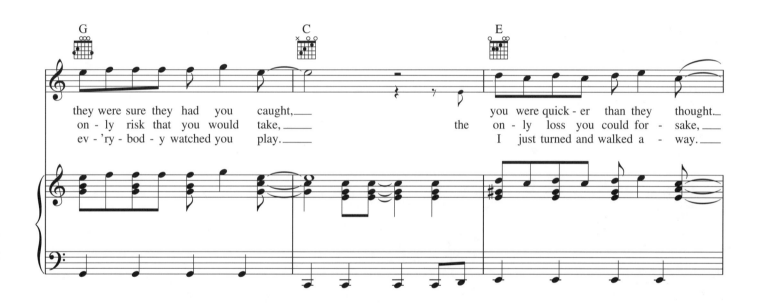

they were sure they had you caught,___
on - ly risk that you would take,___
ev - 'ry - bod - y watched you play.___

you were quick - er than they thought.___
the on - ly loss you could for - sake,___
I just turned and walked a - way.___

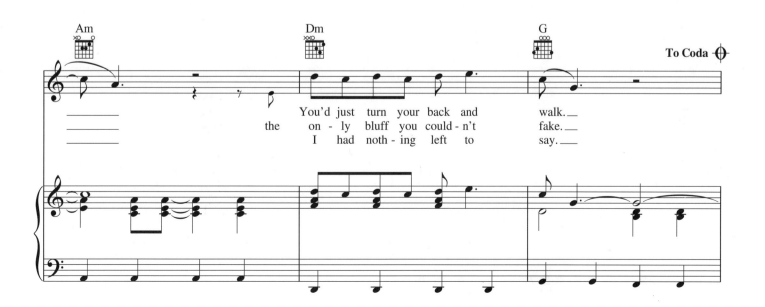

You'd just turn your back and walk.___
the on - ly bluff you could - n't fake.___
I had noth - ing left to say.___

To Coda ⊕

You're still the same.

You still aim high.

D.S. al Coda

CODA

And you're still the same.

And you're still the same.
Mov - in' game to game.
Some things nev - er change.
And you're still the same.

Repeat and Fade

The Stranger

Words and Music by Billy Joel

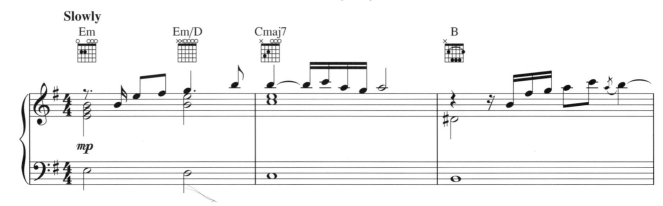

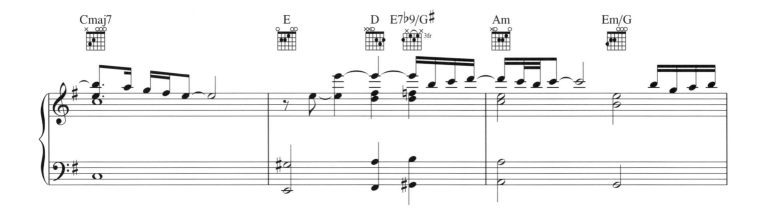

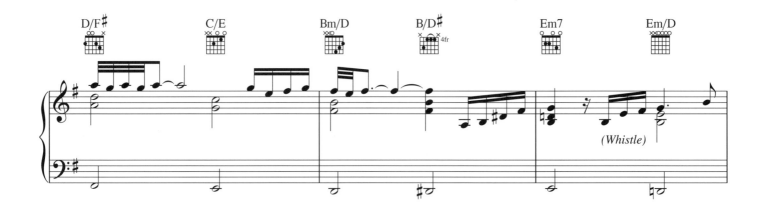

(Whistle)

Well we all have a face _____ That we

Superman (It's Not Easy)

Words and Music by John Ondrasik

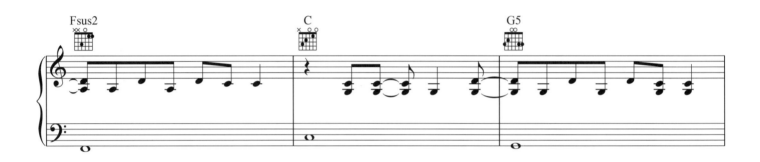

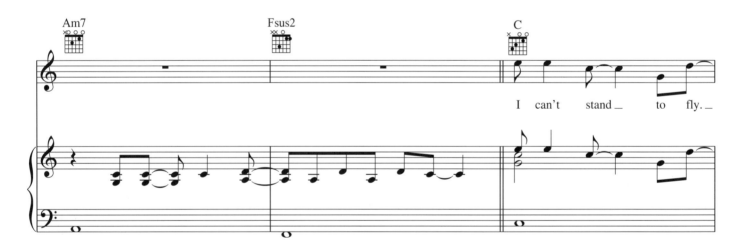

I can't stand __ to fly. __

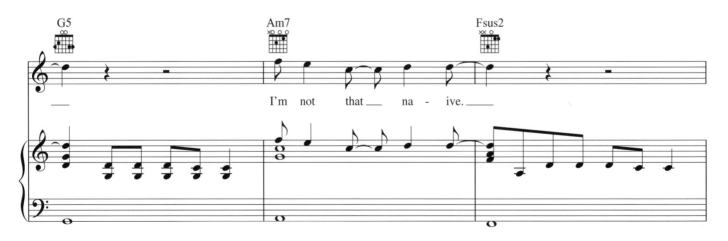

__ I'm not that __ na - ive. __

A Thousand Miles

Words and Music by Vanessa Carlton

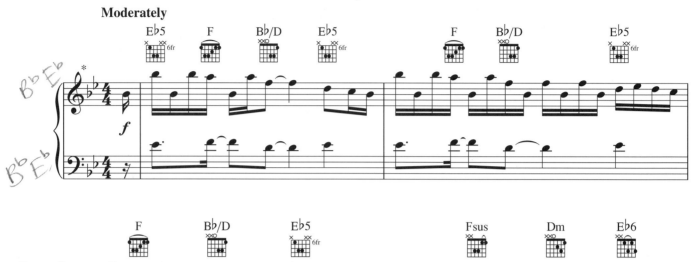

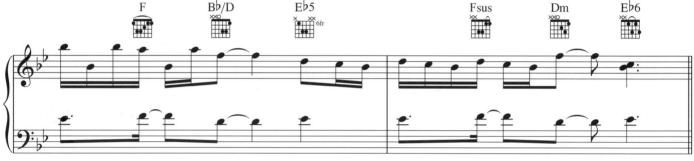

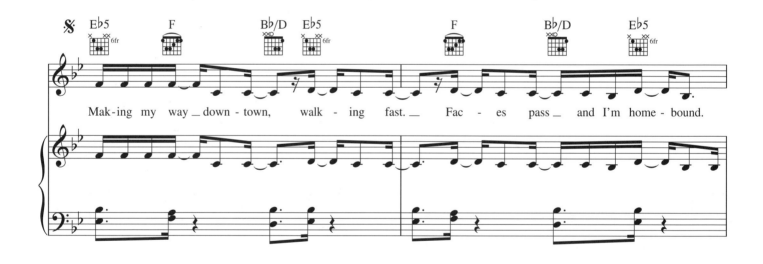

Mak-ing my way _ down-town, walk-ing fast. _ Fac - es pass _ and I'm home-bound.

* Recorded a half step higher.

Walking in Memphis

Words and Music by Marc Cohn

mid-dle of the pour - ing rain.___ Touched down___ in the land of the

Del - ta Blues___ in the mid - dle of the pour - ing rain.

You Are So Beautiful

Words and Music by Billy Preston and Bruce Fisher

Moderately slow, expressively

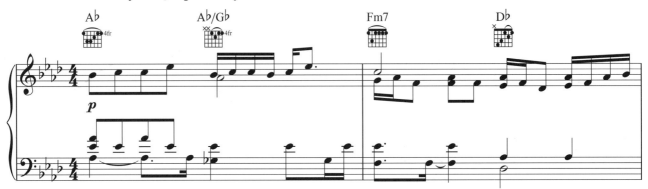

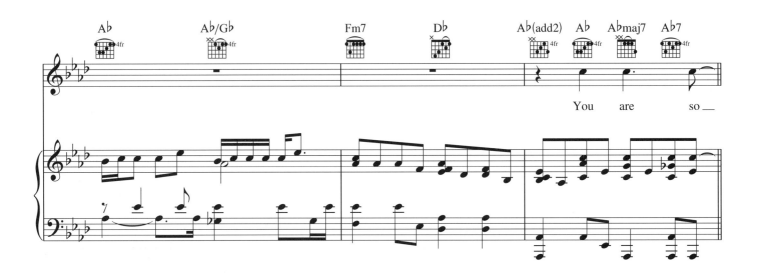

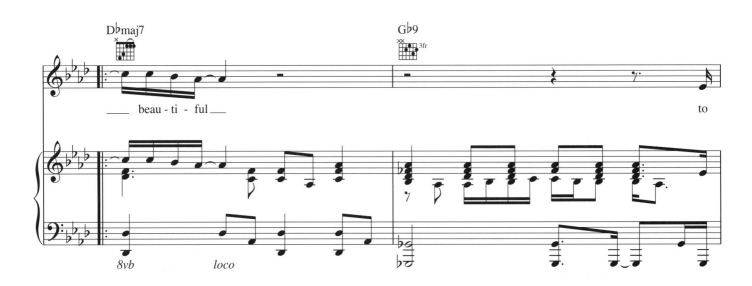

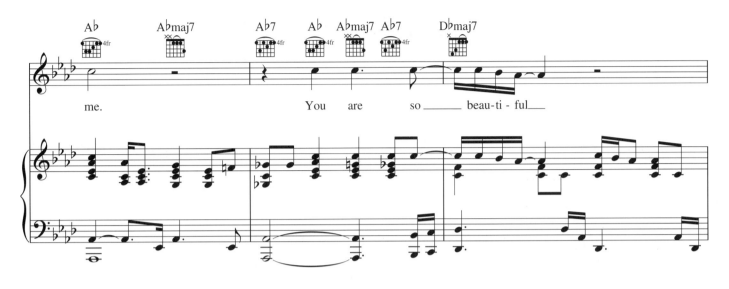

me.

You are so ____ beau-ti - ful ____

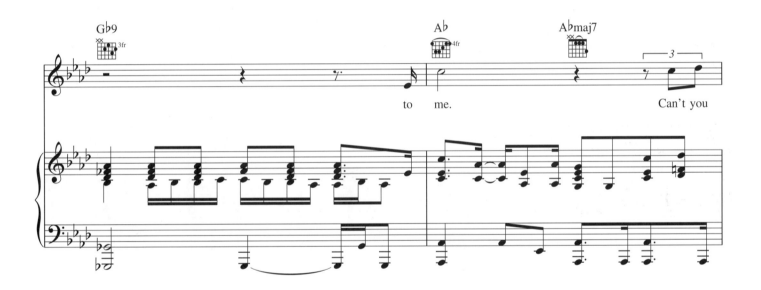

to me.

Can't you

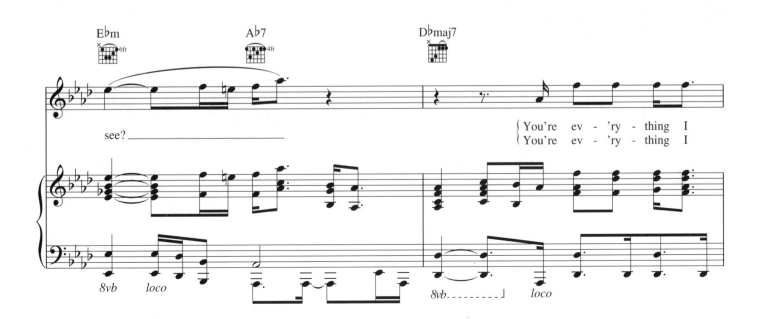

see? ____

You're ev - 'ry - thing I
You're ev - 'ry - thing I

8vb *loco*

8vb *loco*

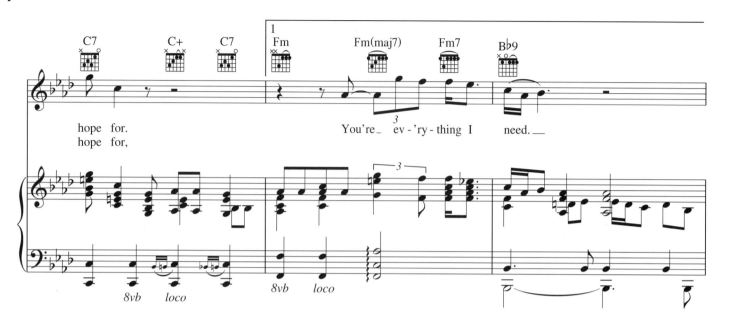

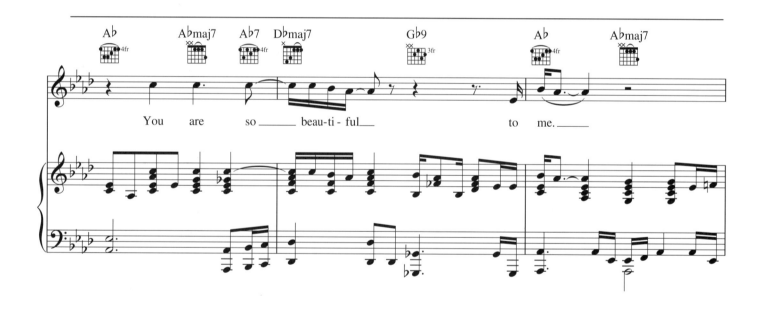

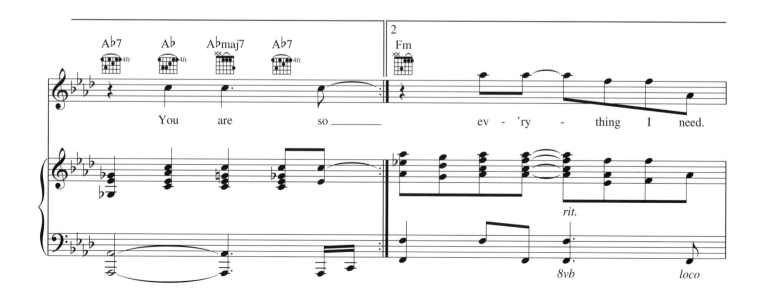

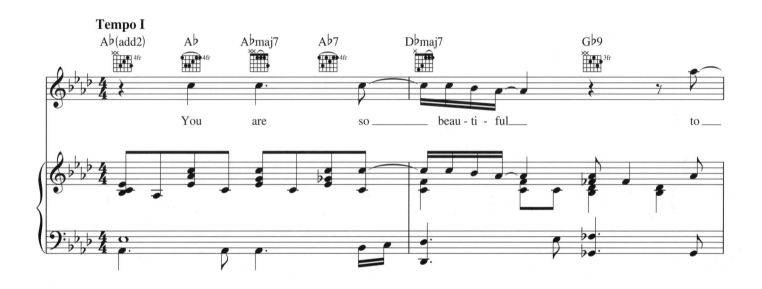

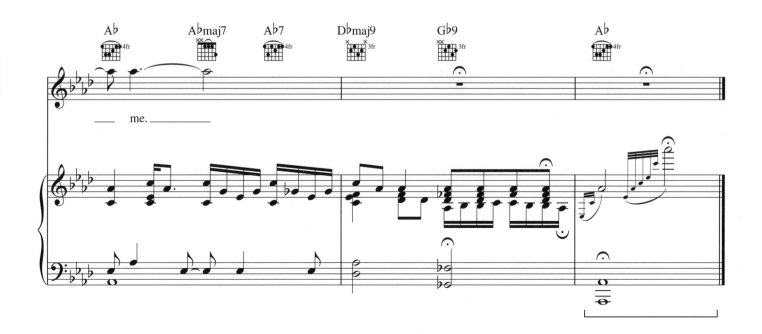

You Are the Sunshine of My Life

Words and Music by Stevie Wonder

THE POP/ROCK ERA

Hal Leonard is proud to present these fantastic folios that gather the best popular songs from the '50s to today! All books arranged for piano, voice, and guitar.

THE POP/ROCK ERA: THE '50s

54 highlights from the first official decade of the pop/rock revolution, including: All Shook Up • At the Hop • Don't Be Cruel (To a Heart That's True) • Donna • Get a Job • Great Balls of Fire • Hound Dog • It's So Easy • Kansas City • (You've Got) Personality • That'll Be the Day • Why Do Fools Fall in Love • and more.
00310788..$14.95

THE POP/ROCK ERA: THE '60s

52 songs that helped shape the pop/rock era, including: Baby Love • Can't Take My Eyes off of You • Crying • Fun, Fun, Fun • Hey Jude • I Heard It Through the Grapevine • I Think We're Alone Now • Louie, Louie • Mony, Mony • Respect • Stand by Me • Stop! In the Name of Love • Wooly Bully • and more.
00310789..$14.95

THE POP/ROCK ERA: THE '70s

44 of the top songs from the '70s, including: ABC • Baby, I Love Your Way • Bohemian Rhapsody • Don't Cry Out Loud • Fire and Rain • I Love the Night Life • Imagine • Joy to the World • Just My Imagination (Running Away with Me) • The Logical Song • Oye Como Va • Piano Man • Three Times a Lady • We've Only Just Begun • You Are So Beautiful • and more.
00310790..$14.95

THE POP/ROCK ERA: THE '80s

38 top pop hits from the '80s, including: Back in the High Life Again • Centerfold • Every Breath You Take • Eye in the Sky • Higher Love •Summer of '69 • Sweet Dreams (Are Made of This) • Thriller • Time After Time • and more.
0031079..$14.95

THE POP/ROCK ERA: THE '90s

35 hits that shaped pop music in the 1990s, including: All I Wanna Do • Angel • Come to My Window • (Everything I Do) I Do It for You • Fields of Gold • From a Distance • Hard to Handle • Hero • I Will Remember You • Mambo No. 5 (A Little Bit Of...) • My Heart Will Go On (Love Theme from 'Titanic') • Ray of Light • Tears in Heaven • When She Cries • and more.
00310792..$14.95

FOR MORE INFORMATION, SEE YOUR LOCAL MUSIC DEALER, OR WRITE TO:

HAL•LEONARD® CORPORATION

7777 W. BLUEMOUND RD. P.O. BOX 13819 MILWAUKEE, WI 53213

www.halleonard.com

HAL•LEONARD
ESSENTIAL SONGS

Play the best songs from the Roaring '20s to today! Each collection features dozens of the most memorable songs of each decade, or in your favorite musical style, arranged in piano/vocal/guitar format.

THE 1920s

Over 100 songs that shaped the decade: Ain't We Got Fun? • Basin Street Blues • Bye Bye Blackbird • Can't Help Lovin' Dat Man • I Wanna Be Loved by You • Makin' Whoopee • Ol' Man River • Puttin' On the Ritz • Toot, Toot, Tootsie • Yes Sir, That's My Baby • and more.

00311200 ....$24.95

THE 1930s

97 essential songs from the 1930s: April in Paris • Body and Soul • Cheek to Cheek • Falling in Love with Love • Georgia on My Mind • Heart and Soul • I'll Be Seeing You • The Lady Is a Tramp • Mood Indigo • My Funny Valentine • You Are My Sunshine • and more.

00311193 ....$24.95

THE 1940s

An amazing collection of over 100 songs from the '40s: Boogie Woogie Bugle Boy • Don't Get Around Much Anymore • Have I Told You Lately That I Love You • I'll Remember April • Route 66 • Sentimental Journey • Take the "A" Train • You'd Be So Nice to Come Home To • and more.

00311192 ....$24.95

THE 1950s

Over 100 pivotal songs from the 1950s, including: All Shook Up • Bye Bye Love • Chantilly Lace • Fever • Great Balls of Fire • Kansas City • Love and Marriage • Mister Sandman • Rock Around the Clock • Sixteen Tons • Tennessee Waltz • Wonderful! Wonderful! • and more.

00311191 ....$24.95

THE 1960s

104 '60s essentials, including: Baby Love • California Girls • Dancing in the Street • Hey Jude • I Heard It Through the Grapevine • Respect • Stand by Me • Twist and Shout • Will You Love Me Tomorrow • Yesterday • You Keep Me Hangin' On and more.

00311190 ....$24.95

THE 1970s

Over 80 of the best songs from the '70s: American Pie • Band on the Run • Come Sail Away • Dust in the Wind • I Feel the Earth Move • Let It Be • Morning Has Broken • Smoke on the Water • Take a Chance on Me • The Way We Were • You're So Vain • and more.

00311189 ....$24.95

THE 1980s

Over 70 classics from the age of power pop and hair metal: Against All Odds • Call Me • Ebony and Ivory • The Heat Is On • Jump • Manic Monday • Sister Christian • Time After Time • Up Where We Belong • What's Love Got to Do with It • and more.

00311188 ....$24.95

THE 1990s

68 songs featuring country-crossover, swing revival, the birth of grunge, and more: Change the World • Fields of Gold • Ironic • Livin' La Vida Loca • More Than Words • Smells like Teen Spirit • Walking in Memphis • Zoot Suit Riot • and more.

00311187 ....$24.95

THE 2000s

59 of the best songs that brought in the new millennium: Accidentally in Love • Beautiful • Don't Know Why • Get the Party Started • Hey Ya! • I Hope You Dance • 1985 • This Love • A Thousand Miles • Wherever You Will Go • Who Let the Dogs Out • You Raise Me Up • and more.

00311186...........................$24.95

BROADWAY

Over 90 songs of the stage: Any Dream Will Do • Blue Skies • Cabaret • Don't Cry for Me, Argentina • Edelweiss • Hello, Dolly! • I'll Be Seeing You • Memory • The Music of the Night • Oklahoma • Summer Nights • There's No Business Like Show Business • Tomorrow • more.

00311222...........................$24.95

CHRISTMAS

Over 100 essential holiday favorites: Blue Christmas • The Christmas Song • Deck the Hall • Frosty the Snow Man • Joy to the World • Merry Christmas, Darling • Rudolph the Red-Nosed Reindeer • Silver Bells • and more!

00311241 ....$24.95

JAZZ STANDARDS

99 jazz classics no music library should be without: Autumn in New York • Body and Soul • Don't Get Around Much Anymore • Easy to Love (You'd Be So Easy to Love) • I've Got You Under My Skin • The Lady Is a Tramp • Mona Lisa • Satin Doll • Stardust • Witchcraft • and more.

00311226 ....$24.95

LOVE SONGS

Over 80 romantic hits: Can You Feel the Love Tonight • Endless Love • From This Moment On • Have I Told You Lately • I Just Called to Say I Love You • Love Will Keep Us Together • My Heart Will Go On • Wonderful Tonight • You Are So Beautiful • more.

00311235 ....$24.95

MOVIE SONGS

94 of the most popular silver screen songs: Alfie • Beauty and the Beast • Chariots of Fire • Footloose • I Will Remember You • Jailhouse Rock • Moon River • People • Somewhere Out There • Summer Nights • Unchained Melody • and more.

00311236 ....$24.95

TV SONGS

Over 100 terrific tube tunes, including: The Addams Family Theme • Bonanza • The Brady Bunch • Desperate Housewives Main Title • I Love Lucy • Law and Order • Linus and Lucy • Sesame Street Theme • Theme from the Simpsons • Theme from the X-Files • and more!

00311223 ....$24.95

THE TWENTIETH CENTURY SERIES

This beautiful series of songbooks celebrates the first century of recorded music and the many genres of music that evolved over 100 years. Each book is arranged for piano and voice with guitar chord frames.

THE 20TH CENTURY:
BROADWAY

A comprehensive overview of 100 years of Broadway musicals with over 70 songs, including: Ain't Misbehavin' • And All That Jazz • As If We Never Said Goodbye • Beauty and the Beast • Brotherhood of Man • Cabaret • Close Every Door • Give My Regards to Broadway • Hello, Dolly! • I'd Give My Life for You • The Impossible Dream (The Quest) • On My Own • One • Seasons of Love • Some Enchanted Evening • Song on the Sand (La Da Da Da) • The Surrey with the Fringe on Top • and more!

_____00310693 ....$19.95

THE 20TH CENTURY:
COUNTRY MUSIC

Over 70 country classics representative of a century's worth of music, including: All the Gold in California • Always on My Mind • Amazed • Blue • Blue Eyes Crying in the Rain • Blue Moon of Kentucky • Boot Scootin' Boogie • Breathe • Could I Have This Dance • Crazy • Folsom Prison Blues • Friends in Low Places • Harper Valley P.T.A. • Hey, Good Lookin' • Jambalaya (On the Bayou) • King of the Road • Lucille • Ring of Fire • Your Cheatin' Heart • and more.

_____00310673 ....$19.95

THE 20TH CENTURY:
JAZZ STANDARDS

Over 70 jazz standards that set the tone for the 20th century, including: All or Nothing at All • Autumn in New York • Body and Soul • Brazil • Caravan • Don't Get Around Much Anymore • Harlem Nocturne • How Deep Is the Ocean (How High Is the Sky) • I'm Beginning to See the Light • In the Mood • Manhattan • Misty • Route 66 • Satin Doll • Skylark • Slightly Out of Tune (Desafinado) • Star Dust • Stella by Starlight • Take the "A" Train • and more!

_____00310696 ....$19.95

THE 20TH CENTURY:
LOVE SONGS

Over 60 of the century's favorite love songs, including: Always in My Heart (Siempre en mi corazón) • And I Love Her • Cherish • (They Long to Be) Close to You • Just the Way You Are • Make It with You • (You Make Me Feel Like) A Natural Woman • Star Dust • Unexpected Song • The Very Thought of You • When I Fall in Love • Wonderful Tonight • You Are the Sunshine of My Life • You Needed Me • You've Got a Friend • more.

_____00310698 ....$19.95

THE 20TH CENTURY:
MOVIE MUSIC

Over 60 of the century's best songs from the cinema, including: Be a Clown • Change the World • Chariots of Fire • Do You Know Where You're Going To? • Endless Love • Footloose • Hakuna Matata • I Will Remember You • Love Story • Moon River • My Heart Will Go On (Love Theme from 'Titanic') • Supercalifragilisticexpialidocious • Tears in Heaven • Unchained Melody • The Way We Were • more.

_____00310694 ....$19.95

THE 20TH CENTURY:
THE ROCK ERA

Over 60 songs that defined the rock era, including: Baby Love • Bohemian Rhapsody • Dancing in the Street • Dust in the Wind • Eleanor Rigby • Fire and Rain • Heartbreak Hotel • I Got You (I Feel Good) • Imagine • Layla • Oh, Pretty Woman • Piano Man • Surfin' U.S.A. • Time After Time • Twist and Shout • Wild Thing • more.

_____00310697 ....$19.95

FOR MORE INFORMATION, SEE YOUR LOCAL MUSIC DEALER,
OR WRITE TO:

HAL•LEONARD®
CORPORATION
7777 W. BLUEMOUND RD. P.O.BOX 13819 MILWAUKEE, WI 53213

Visit Hal Leonard Online at
www.halleonard.com

Prices, contents, and availability subject to change without notice.

THE ULTIMATE SERIES

This comprehensive series features jumbo collections of piano/vocal arrangements with guitar chords. Each volume features an outstanding selection of your favorite songs. Collect them all for the ultimate music library!

Blues

90 blues classics, including: Boom Boom • Born Under a Bad Sign • Gee Baby, Ain't I Good to You • I Can't Quit You Baby • Pride and Joy • (They Call It) Stormy Monday • Sweet Home Chicago • Why I Sing the Blues • You Shook Me • and more.

00310723 . . . .$19.95

Broadway Gold

100 show tunes: Beauty and the Beast • Do-Re-Mi • I Whistle a Happy Tune • The Lady Is a Tramp • Memory • My Funny Valentine • Oklahoma • Some Enchanted Evening • Summer Nights • Tomorrow • many more.

00361396 . . . .$21.95

Broadway Platinum

100 popular Broadway show tunes, featuring: Consider Yourself • Getting to Know You • Gigi • Do You Hear the People Sing • I'll Be Seeing You • My Favorite Things • People • She Loves Me • Try to Remember • Younger Than Springtime • many more.

00311496 . . . .$19.95

Children's Songbook

66 fun songs for kids: Alphabet Song • Be Our Guest • Bingo • The Brady Bunch • Do-Re-Mi • Hakuna Matata • It's a Small World • Kum Ba Yah • Sesame Street Theme • Tomorrow • Won't You Be My Neighbor? • and more.

00310690 . . . .$18.95

Christmas – Third Edition

Includes: Carol of the Bells • Deck the Hall • Frosty the Snow Man • Gesu Bambino • Good King Wenceslas • Jingle-Bell Rock • Joy to the World • Nuttin' for Christmas • O Holy Night • Rudolph the Red-Nosed Reindeer • Silent Night • What Child Is This? • and more.

00361399 . . . .$19.95

Classic Rock

70 rock classics in one great collection! Includes: Angie • Best of My Love • California Girls • Crazy Little Thing Called Love • I Love Rock'N'Roll • Joy to the World • Landslide • Light My Fire • Livin' on a Prayer • Mony, Mony • (She's) Some Kind of Wonderful • Sultans of Swing • Sweet Emotion • Werewolves of London • Wonderful Tonight • Ziggy Stardust • and more.

00310962 . . . .$22.95

Country – Second Edition

90 of your favorite country hits: Boot Scootin' Boogie • Chattahoochie • Could I Have This Dance • Crazy • Down at the Twist And Shout • Hey, Good Lookin' • Lucille • When She Cries • and more.

00310036 . . . .$19.95

Early Rock 'N' Roll

100 classics, including: All Shook Up • Bye Bye Love • Duke of Earl • Gloria • Hello Mary Lou • It's My Party • Johnny B. Goode • The Loco-Motion • Lollipop • Surfin' U.S.A. • The Twist • Wooly Bully • Yakety Yak • and more.

00361411 . . . .$21.95

Gospel

Includes: El Shaddai • His Eye Is on the Sparrow • How Great Thou Art • Just a Closer Walk With Thee • Lead Me, Guide Me • (There'll Be) Peace in the Valley (For Me) • Precious Lord, Take My Hand • Wings of a Dove • more.

00241009 . . . .$19.95

Jazz Standards

Over 100 great jazz favorites: Ain't Misbehavin' • All of Me • Come Rain or Come Shine • Here's That Rainy Day • I'll Take Romance • Imagination • Li'l Darlin' • Manhattan • Moonglow • Moonlight in Vermont • A Night in Tunisia • The Party's Over • Solitude • Star Dust • and more.

00361407 . . . .$19.95

Latin Songs

80 hot Latin favorites, including: Amapola (Pretty Little Poppy) • Amor • Bésame Mucho (Kiss Me Much) • Blame It on the Bossa Nova • Feelings (¿Dime?) • Malaguena • Mambo No. 5 • Perfidia • Slightly out of Tune (Desafinado) • What a Diff'rence a Day Made • more.

00310689 . . . .$19.95

Love and Wedding Songbook

90 songs of devotion including: The Anniversary Waltz • Canon in D • Endless Love • Forever and Ever, Amen • Just the Way You Are • Love Me Tender • Sunrise, Sunset • Through the Years • Trumpet Voluntary • and more!

00361445 . . . .$19.95

Movie Music

73 favorites from the big screen, including: Can You Feel the Love Tonight • Chariots of Fire • Cruella De Vil • Driving Miss Daisy • Easter Parade • Forrest Gump • Moon River • That Thing You Do! • Viva Las Vegas • The Way We Were • When I Fall in Love • and more.

00310240 . . . .$18.95

FOR MORE INFORMATION, SEE YOUR LOCAL MUSIC DEALER, OR WRITE TO:

HAL•LEONARD®
CORPORATION

7777 W. BLUEMOUND RD. P.O. BOX 13819 MILWAUKEE, WI 53213

http://www.halleonard.com

Prices, contents, and availability subject to change without notice. Availability and pricing may vary outside the U.S.A.

Nostalgia Songs

100 great favorites from yesteryear, such as: Ain't We Got Fun? • Alexander's Ragtime Band • Casey Jones • Chicago • Danny Boy • Second Hand Rose • Swanee • Toot, Toot, Tootsie! • 'Way Down Yonder in New Orleans • The Yellow Rose of Texas • You Made Me Love You • and more!

00310730 . . . .$17.95

Pop/Rock

70 of the most popular pop/rock hits of our time, including: Bad, Bad Leroy Brown • Bohemian Rhapsody • Complicated • Drops of Jupiter (Tell Me) • Dust in the Wind • Every Little Thing She Does Is Magic • (Everything I Do) I Do It for You • From a Distance • I Don't Want to Wait • I Will Remember You • Imagine • Invisible Touch • More Than Words • Smooth • Tears in Heaven • Thriller • Walking in Memphis • You Are So Beautiful • and more.

00310963 . . . .$22.95

Singalong!

100 of the best-loved popular songs ever: Beer Barrel Polka • Crying in the Chapel • Edelweiss • Feelings • Five Foot Two, Eyes of Blue • For Me and My Gal • Indiana • It's a Small World • Que Sera, Sera • This Land Is Your Land • When Irish Eyes Are Smiling • and more.

00361418 . . . .$18.95

Standard Ballads

91 mellow masterpieces, including: Angel Eyes • Body and Soul • Darn That Dream • Day By Day • Easy to Love • Isn't It Romantic? • Misty • Mona Lisa • Moon River • My Funny Valentine • Smoke Gets in Your Eyes • When I Fall in Love • and more.

00310246 . . . .$19.95

Swing Standards

93 songs to get you swinging, including: Bandstand Boogie • Boogie Woogie Bugle Boy • Heart and Soul • How High the Moon • In the Mood • Moonglow • Satin Doll • Sentimental Journey • Witchcraft • and more.

00310245 . . . .$19.95

TV Themes

More than 90 themes from your favorite TV shows, including: The Addams Family Theme • Cleveland Rocks • Theme from Frasier • Happy Days • Love Boat Theme • Hey, Hey We're the Monkees • Nadia's Theme • Sesame Street Theme • Theme from Star Trek® • and more.

00310841 . . . .$19.95